Contents

Notes on contributors

Stephen Baron is Director of Research at the Faculty of Education, University of Glasgow. A former Raising of the School Leaving Age (RoSLa) and remedial teacher, his research interests are in the cultural studies of education, particularly the reproduction of marginal groups. He has published widely on the politics of education and of community and is currently completing *The politics of learning disability* with Paul Dumbleton (Macmillan, 2000: forthcoming).

Professor Frank Coffield has been Professor of Education in the Department of Education at the University of Newcastle since April 1996, having previously worked at Durham and Keele Universities. He is currently Director of the ESRC's research programme into *The Learning Society* from 1994 to 2000. In 1997 he edited a report *A national strategy for lifelong learning* (Department of Education, University of Newcastle) and produced in 1999 *Breaking the consensus: Lifelong learning as social control* (Department of Education, University of Newcastle).

Dr Pat Davies is Reader in Continuing Education at City University, London and has published widely in the field of access and participation of adults in education and training. She is also a co-director of the project 'The impact of credit-based learning systems on learning cultures', which is part of the ESRC's *The Learning Society Programme*.

Professor Michael Eraut is Professor of Education at the University of Sussex Institute of Education. He directed one of the projects entitled 'Development of knowledge and skills in employment', as part of the ESRC's *The Learning Society Programme*. He has published widely in the areas of professional and vocational education and about different types of knowledge.

Professor Ralph Fevre is Professor of Social Research at Cardiff University, having previously held various posts in the University of Wales since 1982. He recently edited (with Andrew Thompson) a volume of articles on *Nation, identity and social theory* (University of Wales Press, 1999) and forthcoming titles include *The demoralisation of western culture* (Continuum, 2000) and *The sociology of economic behaviour* (Sage Publications, 2001).

Professor John Field is Professor of Lifelong Learning at the University of Warwick, where he chairs the Department of Continuing Education. Previously he worked in the School of Education, University of Ulster. He has published widely on lifelong learning, vocational training and adult education. His most recent book is *European dimensions: Education, training and the European Union* (Jessica Kingsley, 1998).

Stephen Gorard is a senior lecturer at the School of Social Sciences, Cardiff University. His research interests include lifelong learning, the impact of schools on attainment, the impact of markets on education, and the role of technology in widening educational participation. He is currently working on projects relating to the last two of these, funded by the ESRC and the Spencer Foundation respectively.

Professor Gareth Rees is Professor and Deputy Director in the Cardiff University School of Social Sciences. He has researched and published widely on lifelong learning, vocational education and training and regional economic development and the governance of education policy. He is currently a consultant to the Organisation of Economic Cooperation and Development (OECD) on 'Learning cities and regions'.

Professor Sheila Riddell worked as Research Fellow in the Department of Education, University of Edinburgh following her PhD at Bristol University in 1988. From 1989 to 1996 she taught and researched at Stirling University and was promoted to Personal Chair in 1995. After a period as Dean of Arts and Social Science at Napier University, Edinburgh, Sheila took up the post of Professor of Social Policy (Disability Studies) at Glasgow University where she is Director of the Strathclyde Centre for Disability Research. She has researched and written extensively in the areas of special educational needs/disability and gender and education.

Lynda Spence has worked as a Research Officer at the University of Ulster on a number of projects, including 'Divergence between initial and continuing education in Scotland and Northern Ireland', one of the projects within *The Learning Society Programme*. She is currently a research consultant to the voluntary sector in Northern Ireland.

Alastair Wilson is Research Fellow in the Strathclyde Centre for Disability Research, University of Glasgow. After a period as a husky handler he graduated in History from the University of Glasgow where he also trained as an adult education worker. His research interests are in disability and learning difficulties, particularly the development of supported employment schemes.

The structure below the surface: reassessing the significance of informal learning

Frank Coffield

Introduction

If all learning were to be represented by an iceberg, then the section above the surface of the water would be sufficient to cover formal learning, but the submerged two thirds of the structure would be needed to convey the much greater importance of informal learning. That, briefly, is the growing conviction of a subgroup of researchers within the Economic and Social Research Council's (ESRC) programme of research into The Learning Society. When the programme was first commissioned in 1995, none of the 14 projects was funded to study informal learning as its central focus. However, as internal meetings of the project directors got underway and debates began, it became increasingly clear from an examination of the data from a number of projects that informal learning was much more significant than many of us had previously recognised. So a conference dedicated to this theme was organised, papers were presented and this report is the outcome of those endeavours.

However, there has been no parallel shift in the thinking of government, employers, practitioners or most researchers. This report, unashamedly more historical and more theoretical than its three predecessors in this ESRC Learning Society series from The Policy Press, is dedicated to encouraging a deep change in attitude.

The two most relevant government reports – *The Learning Age* (DfEE, 1997) and *Learning to succeed* (DfEE, 1999) – both ignore informal learning and continue their heavy emphasis on formal provision, qualifications and accountability. The nation's progress towards creating a learning society is therein measured by National Learning Targets, which are defined by the percentages of individuals attaining particular qualifications, and by the ability of education institutions to widen access, improve retention and increase the proportion of students who complete courses.

In a similar vein, the language of employers refers to the need for "a skills revolution" (CBI, 1989), "world class targets" (CBI, 1991) and a "skills passport" (CBI, 1995). These reports argue for "core" and "transferable skills", for a "coherent qualifications framework" and for changes in the funding regime. Again, exclusive attention is paid to the provision of formal education and training.

This report, in contrast, breaks away from the standard, mainstream approach to learning and argues instead that formal education and training represent only a small part of all the learning that goes on in schools, colleges, at work, at home and in the community. It goes further by claiming that, although informal learning is routinely ignored by government, employers and most researchers, it is often necessary, whereas formal training is often dispensable. The five chapters in this report explore different aspects of the submerged and neglected world of informal learning. Taken together, they amount to a plea for a fundamental reassessment of its significance.

However, this report should not be misinterpreted as claiming to be the first to have 'discovered' the significance of informal learning. The long tradition of anthropological studies of informal, everyday learning is here acknowledged, a tradition which includes the more recent arguments of Lave and Wenger (1991) against sharp dichotomies such as 'formal' and 'informal' learning. Their study wrestles with the puzzle of how learning takes place without teaching and how apprenticeships can be organised within communities both formally and informally. Within adult education, Tough (1979) demonstrated more than 20 years ago that most adults regularly undertake self-directed learning 'projects' outside of school or work-based training. It seems that the significance of informal learning is recognised, then promptly forgotten and then rediscovered some years later. There is a strong tendency for policy makers, researchers and practitioners to admit readily the importance of informal learning and then to proceed to develop policy, theory and practice without further reference to it. We must move beyond this periodic genuflection in the direction of informal learning and incorporate it into plans for a learning society.

At a personal level, a few moments reflection is sufficient to gauge the relative importance of formal and informal education. In my own case, it was in informal settings where I first heard 'the facts of life', where I first learned how to treat a girl on a date, where I found out how much alcohol I could safely consume. As I grew up, the role of informal learning in my education increased, with politics, religion, literature, music and football all being debated late into the night with my contemporaries.

Recommendations from friends about new novels, records, and courses were treated as 'hot' knowledge, compared with the coolness with which reference lists or advice from most tutors were received. It is only a slight exaggeration to say that during my years at Glasgow University I learned more in beer bars than I did in lecture halls and would have learned much more if the former had not closed at 9.30pm in Scotland in the early 1960s. Informal learning, then, may play the psychological role of engaging students of all ages in learning and helping some of them to survive formal education. For me it acted as an indispensable complement to, rather than an easy replacement of, formal knowledge.

Kumar argues that informal learning should no longer be dismissed as extra-curricular, but:

... must come to be seen and attended to as the real heart of university life and the main justification of the university's existence ... universities were – and are – unique concentrations of a diversity of talents formed by family, school and class cultures. They provide the milieu in which these talents find the space and opportunity to flourish, often in areas remote from the formal academic curriculum. It is in this, rather than in the provision of formal learning, that the universities are distinctive. It has often struck many of us who work in universities that the students learn more from each other, in a variety of ways, than they do from us: purveyors indeed of increasingly questioned and questionable stocks of knowledge. (Kumar, 1997, pp 28-9)

The main theme of this report is to examine informal learning in a wide variety of contexts. In Northern Ireland, for example, John Field and Lynda Spence claim in Chapter 2 that relatively low levels of participation in formal education and training for adults can "simply mean that people have found that informal learning is a better way of achieving the goals they set themselves". Stephen Baron, Alastair Wilson and Sheila Riddell in Chapter 3 studied the provision of supported employment for adults with learning difficulties and argue that "becoming a competent member of the workplace depends less on formally defined skills and their acquisition through training than on scarcely noticed processes of acculturation into social networks and their whole ways of life". For Pat Davies, studying a highly successful system of credits for non-traditional learners in London, the concern is that certification may destroy the highly motivating informality between tutor and student and may even alienate the latter. Thankfully, the empirical data that she explores in Chapter 4 showed that such fears were largely unfounded. Finally, in a long Chapter 5, Ralph Fevre, Stephen Gorard and Gareth Rees draw on an historical archive to suggest that in South Wales, prior to mechanisation in the first half of the 20th century, there was an informal system of training in coal-mining in the region which formed knowledge and skills more effectively than a more formal system might have. In the second half of their paper, they use their survey of more than one thousand residents and in-depth interviews with 10% of them to make the provocative suggestion that "formal training may lead to unnecessary learning whereas informal learning is concerned with the acquisition of necessary knowledge and skills".

The nature of the first chapter in this collection is rather different. In a long, theoretical exposition, which remains clear and accessible throughout, Michael Eraut breaks new ground by providing a fresh set of definitions of the main terms under consideration, a typology of non-formal learning, a detailed analysis of tacit knowledge (of people and of contexts and of tacit knowledge in action) as well as a useful critique of interpretations of situated learning which seek to collectivise all personal knowledge. He begins by arguing that the term 'non-formal learning' should be preferred as the contrast to formal learning rather than the term 'informal learning' because the adjective 'informal' is used colloquially to describe, for example, dress, meetings or personal style which may have little to do with learning per se. He continues by offering a typology of non-formal learning and provides a new framework and a language which other researchers within *The Learning Society Programme* then drew upon to make better sense of these issues, thereby illustrating a growing coordination within the programme. It is every editor's wish to receive as a contribution a masterly overview, a *tour d'horizon*, which will be used and debated for years to come because it makes theoretical advances. Michael Eraut's is such a seminal chapter.

The Learning Society Programme

Before further discussion of the main themes running through all five chapters, it is appropriate to introduce briefly *The Learning Society Programme*. The full title of the programme is *The Learning Society: Knowledge and skills for employment* and the original specification described it as follows:

> The programme is a response to the growing national consensus that the UK needs to transform radically its thinking and practice in relation to education and training if it is to survive as a major economic power with a high quality of life, political freedom and social justice for all its citizens.
>
> The aim of the programme is to examine the nature of what has been called a learning society and to explore the ways in which it can contribute to the development of knowledge and skills for employment and other areas of adult life. The programme focuses on post-compulsory education, training and continuing education in a wide variety of contexts, both formal and informal. (ESRC, Research Specification, 1994)

The programme consists of 14 projects, involving more than 50 researchers in teams spread throughout the UK from Belfast to Brighton. Each project has a different starting and finishing time and the programme itself will run until March 2000.

The present volume is the last in a series of four reports published by The Policy Press in 1998/2000 on such themes as skill formation (the topic of the first report[1]), studies of lifelong learning in Europe (the topic of the second[2]) and of research and policy on lifelong learning (the third report[3]). *The Learning Society Programme* has also produced a contribution to the public debate on lifelong learning entitled *A national strategy for lifelong learning* (Coffield, 1997); a collection of articles, which explored the concept of a learning society, in a special edition of the *Journal of Education Policy* (vol 12, no 5, November-December 1997); and a critique of government policy on lifelong learning, called *Breaking the consensus: Lifelong learning as social control* (Coffield, 1999). The projects have each also produced for the general reader a brief, two-page summary of their objectives, approach, main findings, policy implications and key publications and sets of these summaries are available[4]. Each project within the Programme will shortly produce a comprehensive overview of their research in two edited collections of articles to be published by The Policy Press in 2000.

What is distinctive about this fourth and last report in the series is that it shows how the projects 'gelled together', a considerable achievement given the very disparate nature of the main topics studied by each team. A collegial atmosphere was gradually created and projects used each other's theoretical and conceptual frameworks to examine their own data, an approach which also served as a means of testing those frameworks. Open debate and constructive criticism improved the quality of thinking of all the participants and *The Learning Society Programme* began to exemplify in its interactions not only the culture of learning which the programme as a whole sought to study and stimulate in society, but also the benefits of coordinated research effort.

The five chapters which make up this collection contain four broad themes and the rest of this introduction is structured around them. These themes are as follows:

- The significance of informal learning calls for a larger vision of the learning society than the current official model.

- Attempts to create a culture of lifelong learning have so rarely been enriched by an historical or comparative understanding that the notion that a more effective learning society existed in the recent past than at present is not even entertained.

- The justification for creating a Learning Age in the UK needs to move beyond repeated calls for further investment in human capital to a consideration of other forms of capital such as cultural capital and, especially, social capital.

- If informal learning were to be seriously addressed, what would be the implications for policy?

A larger vision of The Learning Society

The recent White Paper, *Learning to succeed* (DfEE, 1999) has the courage to admit openly the scale of the challenge facing this country in building a new culture of learning, but it also records some remarkable successes as well as some serious weaknesses. For example, one particular statistic deserves to be more widely known: "the percentage of 17 year olds in maintained school sixth forms achieving at least two GCE A level passes has increased from 30% to 69% over a ten year period" (DfEE, 1999, p 16). Such a sudden rise in performance is not just an instance of "good progress" as the White Paper claims, it is a *transformation* of previous notions of educability. It is important to remember that "the initial design [of A levels] was intended for the more academically inclined pupils among the 'top 20 per cent' of the ability range that the grammar schools recruited" (Edwards, 1997, p 3). Yet almost 70% of 17-year-old

students in maintained schools are now reaching a level of attainment which was thought only a generation ago to be beyond the intellectual capabilities of 80% of all students.

This statistic has been chosen to illustrate the official model of The Learning Society as operationalised by successive governments: an unshakeable determination to drive up accredited standards and performance in all areas of education and training. The vision, as detailed in David Blunkett's memorable Foreword to *The Learning Age*, celebrates the wider contribution that learning has to make in creating a civilised society, developing the spiritual side of our lives and promoting active citizenship (DfEE, 1997, p 7).

But how is that admirable vision to be realised? What are the mechanisms of change? National targets have been set and then raised, access to education institutions is being widened and deepened, qualifications are being reformed, classified and placed in a hierarchy to encourage students to climb to the next stage, league tables have been published, performance-related pay is to be introduced, and external inspection is to be made ever more rigorous and independent to improve quality. This remorseless juggernaut is the vehicle chosen by government to take the UK to the promised land of lifelong learning. Every year this enormous chariot is redesigned, parts are added and the wheels are oiled to ensure that it runs faster and faster. But, as the German proverb has it, what is the point of building up speed if we are not on the right road?

Reassessing the role of informal learning encourages us to stand back and use findings from *The Learning Society Programme* to question some of the central assumptions underlying the official model of progress. For instance, does the pursuit and possession of qualifications instil a love of learning? We shy away from addressing this question because the answer may be too threatening. The research of Stephen Ball and his colleagues in one post-16 education and training market in London pointed to those young people whose identities had been so damaged by 11 years of formal schooling that more education and training is viewed as an "impossible or unpalatable" option (Ball et al, 1999).

Do those who become the successes of the formal system of initial education become lifelong learners? John Field and Lynda Spence's analysis of initial and continuing education in Northern Ireland included in this volume shows that there is no simple causal link. Do adult workers who obtain vocational qualifications in a specific area subsequently improve their work performance in that area? The study by Jenny Hewison and her colleagues of training among National Health Service staff demonstrated that the qualifications required by managers for a particular job were not thought necessary by nurses to *do* that job (Dowswell et al, 1999).

Has the overall level of demand by employers for degrees increased as higher education has expanded? More generally, are British workers becoming overqualified for the jobs they do? Alan Felstead and his colleagues provide robust replies to these questions from their major national survey of skill change in Britain during the last decade, a project which was part of *The Learning Society Programme*:

> *Three out of 10 graduates in 1997 were in jobs for which a degree was not an entry requirement – a level similar to that recorded in 1986. This suggests a deficiency in employer demand and a cost to society in terms of underused (but paid for) human capital resources. The mismatch between the demand and the supply of all qualifications is also alarmingly high – in 1997 around one in five of those holding any qualification reported that no qualification at all was required for the job they currently had. (Felstead et al, 1999, p 69)*

Perhaps most crucially from the government's own perspective, if by 2002 all the National Learning Targets have been met, will the British economy have closed the large productivity gap with the USA, Germany and France and become a high value-added, high skill economy? A review of research (commissioned by *The Learning Society Programme*) examined the relationship between higher investment in human capital and economic performance and concluded as follows:

> *Higher levels of education and training may be a necessary precondition for greater economic success, but on their own they are not sufficient to ensure that it occurs. They are better seen as simply one part of a much wider matrix of factors that lead to what the*

OECD has dubbed the 'high performance workplace'.... These findings beg important questions about the efficacy of the UK's current emphasis upon boosting the supply of skills, and assuming that the demand for and effective utilisation of increased skills and knowledge can be left to take care of itself. (Brown and Keep, forthcoming, p 22)

Qualifications will continue to perform the important functions of selecting (and rejecting) people for further education or for jobs, of guaranteeing standards to employers and the community, and of opening up opportunities for all those who obtain them. They have also become, as Pat Davies points out in Chapter 4, "the key measuring instrument not only of learners' achievements but also of the effectiveness of professionals and the performance of institutions". However, our qualification-driven system runs the risk of higher participation rates resulting in much education and training being of dubious value because students are intent on increasing their credentials rather than their understanding. Successive governments have also devalued liberal learning (both formal and non-formal) by giving priority (and complete priority in the case of adult education) to provision which results in certificated output. A further problem is accurately described by Michael Young:

> *The current tension in the credentialist model is between the selective role of qualifications which originated in a division of labour based upon a minority of the population being qualified and the demands in a learning society for the majority to be qualified in new and flexible ways. (Young, 1998, p 152)*

Becoming qualified is no longer the unrepeated achievement of the young and has become the lifelong task of all. That sounds like a national lifelong learning sentence but data from the South Wales project, reported in this volume in Chapter 5, encouragingly suggests that it is those who learn informally inside and outside of work who are more likely to engage in lifelong learning. Take, for example, the worker described in Chapter 5 by Ralph Fevre and his colleagues:

> *One man for whom there was little separation between home and work had taught himself pottery (with his wife), electrolysis for metallising, simple electronics, wax*

casting and furniture modelling. He had a perspex cutting room in his house, a silver-plated frog in his living room, and once made a scale model of the Challenger space shuttle which is now on the desk of a four star general in NASA.

Without any formal qualifications from school, college or university, this multi-skilled man taught himself new trades such as French polishing as a sideline while working as a printer and so kept himself successfully employed. Such "learning entrepreneurs" as Michael Eraut calls them are not rare, remarkable individuals. Ralph Fevre et al provide a number of instances, such as the steel foundryman, a self-taught plasterer and electrician, who learned the skills of bricklaying and of caring for the 7,000 bedding plants in his garden through reading. The strong argument made by both Ralph Fevre et al and Michael Eraut is not just that all this valuable, informal learning is necessary for the fulfilment of the individuals concerned but that it is also vital for the organisations they work for. As Ralph Fevre et al comment, "It is almost as if the best sort of learning – and not simply that very basic learning without which the organisation could not function – is the informal type".

In addition to the so-called transferable skills of literacy, numeracy and information technology (IT), what employers need are employees who have learned how to learn and who wish to go on learning. The significance of these research findings is that a capacity and enthusiasm for learning appears to be transferable between 'useless' and 'useful' knowledge.

These findings show that this type of learning is not trivial and amounts to far more than the acquisition of additional information; it meets the definition proposed by Michael Eraut that "the use of the word 'learning' in the phrase The Learning Society should refer only to significant changes in capability or understanding" (1997, p 556).

An historical perspective

The challenge which informal learning poses to the qualifications industry lies in the fact that many people acquire substantial new skills and knowledge both at work and in their leisure time without any

formal training. One of the many virtues of the South Wales regional study, reported in Chapter 5, is that it provides an historical dimension to this argument by means of taped oral histories of families covering events dating back to 1890. The data shows that before mechanisation and nationalisation new miners learned a range of complex skills, upon which their very lives depended, from an experienced collier "... in an entirely informal system: there were no apprenticeships, no classroom instruction, no paid trainers ... and certainly no certification". This mentoring system worked effectively for many years until the introduction of coal-cutting machines. Later still, nationalisation ushered in a formal training system which included apprenticeships, but the industrial structure of the region was transformed with the closure of the mines: "... the old pattern of informal learning by watching is increasingly inappropriate to the modern manufacturing environment".

However, the surprising finding from their survey of more than 1,000 residents is that "most new jobs involved no training of any type, not even a half-day of Health and Safety training ... new tasks were picked up through 'common sense'" and "the conclusions that most of these respondents drew from their experiences was that, in their view, formal training was unnecessary and that experience was everything". Again, informants spoke eloquently of the greater importance in their lives of the informal learning which took place in transient social interactions inside and outside employment. It is via informal learning that most of us pick up "the deeply implicit rules of the workplace", which prove such a barrier to adults with learning difficulties, as Stephen Baron et al explain in Chapter 3.

The emergence of social capital

While policy documents in the UK remain wedded to an unquestioning faith in the transformative power of human capital[5], projects within *The Learning Society Programme* began to develop further the notion of social capital and to adapt the concept to the study of lifelong learning[6]. For some, social capital helped them to make sense of their data, although that approach had not been part of their original plan.

Bourdieu was one of the first to use the term "social capital or capital of social relationships" (1977, p 503) to describe the way in which lawyers, doctors and politicians invested in "a capital of honourability and respectability which is often indispensable if one desires to attract clients in socially important positions" (Bourdieu, 1977, p 503). Since then, as John Field and Lynda Spence explain in Chapter 2, the idea has been extended to encompass "the networks, norms and shared sense of trust that are available as resources to any group of actors, and not solely elite groupings".

The notion of social capital is not used uncritically, even though the combination of the positive sounding adjective 'social' with the connotations of investment and profit provided by the noun 'capital' appears to produce a term which none could fault. However, unlike economic capital, too much social capital may not be an unalloyed good. A simple policy of building more and more social capital may be a romantic or nostalgic delusion. As John Field and Lynda Spence argue, "while social capital represents an important set of resources for informal learning, it also has limits and drawbacks". Citing the research of Mark Granovetter in the States, John Field and Lynda Spence claim that strong ties can inhibit, constrain and control: "family-based networks may foster business conservatism and hinder innovation". Pahl has made a similar point about the importance in open societies of intermediate institutions and associations as buffers between the family and the state: "local one-party states can lead to totalitarian islands in a pluralistic system" (1991, p 347).

In the particular case of Northern Ireland, with its two partly segregated religious/ethnic communities, social capital has been used in the past not only to provide security and a sense of identity, but also to manage access to jobs and to legitimate inequalities. It is also the contention of Chapter 2's authors that the relatively high levels of social capital found in the province help to explain the intriguing divergence among adults of high levels of informal learning but low levels of participation in formal education and training. Northern Ireland would benefit from weaker, more inclusive and more open

ties which built bridges between different groups, each of which is held together by strong ties. As so often, the lessons for policy are complex and that is the final theme to be addressed.

Policy implications

The White Paper, *Learning to succeed*, proposes to abolish "the awkward and artificial distinction" (DfEE, 1999, p 48) between vocational and non-vocational qualifications. So far so good, because this change in legislation will allow local Learning Partnerships to develop broader learning programmes such as courses on local history or literature. However, no sooner has this concession been made, than the government reveals its continuing preference for formal, accredited forms of learning and for 'useful' knowledge: "although not all the learning funded by the [Learning and Skills] Council will lead to qualifications, we would expect it to give priority to courses that lead to nationally recognised qualifications and – more generally – to encourage learning towards recognised qualifications" (DfEE, 1999, p 48).

A genuine culture of lifelong learning needs to adopt a very broad definition of learning which includes general education, education for living and for active citizenship; improving the skills of the workforce must not become the only or the overriding goal of policy. Many adults, and especially those who have retired, wish to take a broad range of courses and they neither need nor want a qualification. Insisting that such courses become accredited may alienate these learners. Part of the success of the credit-based system, detailed by Pat Davies in Chapter 4, is that "assessment was never forced on learners; it was always voluntary". As the National Institute for Adult and Continuing Education (NIACE) has commented:

Giving priority to courses leading to nationally recognised qualifications may result in a rush to accredit learning which should not be accredited and general adult education being treated as second class, to be paid for only after the 'important' vocational courses. (NIACE, 1999, p 8)

There exists a recurrent theme in much of the literature on informal learning which does not sit comfortably with the rest of the content. Well-deserved praise for imaginative learning projects in the community tends to be accompanied by an unthinking and unqualified denigration of formal education in public institutions and those who work in them. The modern cliché is that the focus must shift from the school to the learner because "teachers are too often unable to relate learning experiences within school to the wider experiences and cultures in which young people participate" (Bentley, 1998, p 180). No evidence is advanced for this criticism of around 400,000 professionals and no allowance is made for the fact that teachers' work has become seriously constrained by the legal requirements of the National Curriculum and by the demands of accountability. Yet within a few pages the same schools and colleges which have been repeatedly castigated for not being part of the real world are to become "neighbourhood learning centres" and the "hubs of learning networks" (Bentley, 1998, p 183). No indication is given of how this remarkable transformation is to take place unless it is believed that professionals can be chided and brow-beaten into change.

In a similar vein, the White Paper, *Learning to succeed*, contains neither a model of change nor a discussion of implementation; it also fails to appreciate the irreplaceable role of those professionals whom the government needs to implement its proposals. For example, support for "providers" is to be supplied "by rigorous and independent external inspection" (DfEE, 1999, p 44). It will be tragic if this failure to understand the complexities of implementation becomes the rock on which New Labour's education reforms were to founder. After all, our current institutions are the physical embodiment of our predecessors' attempts to widen participation, they are situated within walking distance of those who are to be re-engaged in learning and they are staffed by those on whom change in formal education depends.

The implications for policy that flow from this report on informal learning are of a general rather than a specific nature but they are significant nonetheless. For example, attempts to merge aspects of formal and informal learning, as in the credit-based system described by Pat Davies in Chapter 4, have proved remarkably successful from the perspective of both tutors and students − "our study found no evidence that the formalisation of learning through the introduction of assessment had significantly undermined the informal dimensions of adult education or distorted the learning experience of the participants". Such bridges between formal and informal learning suggest one possible way forward.

The key issues can be summarised as follows:

- The existence, significance and necessity of informal learning needs to be more widely acknowledged by policy makers, practitioners, employers and researchers. Informal learning should no longer be regarded as an inferior form of learning whose main purpose is to act as the precursor of formal learning; it needs to be seen as fundamental, necessary and valuable in its own right, at times directly relevant to employment and at other times not relevant at all.

- We need a greater understanding of informal learning as a means of sparking off curiosity in all types of apparently useless knowledge (at least from an economic perspective) and in all types of formal and informal settings. Such curiosity, when aroused, spills out into all areas of life.

- Formal learning relevant to employment needs to be accredited, but policy (and research) on lifelong learning currently places unjustifiable emphasis and reliance on formal provision and certification: "There is valuable learning that does not lead to qualifications or jobs" (McGivney, 1999, p 87).

- There is more to creating a learning society than continually beating the drum of human capital. The more subtle claims of social capital need to be explored, and robust indicators of informal learning should be developed, including criteria for funding.

- Much could be learned from studying more intensively those learning entrepreneurs, those "individuals who *make a career* of informal learning because learning is part of their wider identities (wider than work, that is); they learn at work because they like to learn everywhere" (Fevre et al, Chapter 5, original emphasis).

- The large role played by tacit knowledge in all aspects of our lives needs to be understood and glib talk of making tacit knowledge explicit only reveals ignorance (see Michael Eraut's chapter for further discussion).

- Given the range, depth and quality of the informal learning uncovered by researchers in this report, "the term 'non-learner' to describe non-participants in formal education should be banned from government publications for psychological reasons" (Eraut, 1999, p 2).

- Emphasising the benefit or usefulness of informal learning is not enough, as can be learned from Peter Alheit. His argument takes us to the political core of the debate over The Learning Society:

The problem is not the 'discovery' and 'acceptance' of informal learning, but rather its EVALUATION ... the newly discovered forms of learning run the risk of being instrumentalised and exploited ... informal learning in modern societies can unfold its quality only if the intermediary locations for learning (companies, organisations and educational institutions) change in parallel, if genuinely new learning organisations and new learning publics come into being. A generally accepted informalisation of learning cannot be achieved without democratisation. (Alheit , 1999, pp 77-8; original emphasis)

David Blunkett in his Foreword to the White Paper argues that "we must place the learner at the heart of the new system" (DfEE, 1999). The learner in question would appear to be an employable adult of working age on a formal course leading to a recognised qualification. The case for informal learning has not only still to be won, it has scarcely begun to be heard[7].

Notes

[1] The first publication in the series, entitled *Learning at work* and published by The Policy Press, contains articles by Michael Eraut et al (on learning from other people at work); David Ashton (on learning in organisations); Peter Scott and Antje Cockrill (on training in the construction industry in Wales and Germany); Reiner Siebert (on Jobrotation); Kari Hadjivassiliou et al (on Continuous Vocational Training); and Stephen Baron et al (on what The Learning Society means for adults with learning difficulties).

[2] The second report, entitled *Why's the beer always*

stronger up North? Studies of lifelong learning in Europe, contains some cross-national observations on lifelong learning by Walter Heinz (Bremen); an article on adult guidance services in Europe by Teresa Rees and Will Bartlett; a chapter on different models of Continuous Vocational Training in the UK, France and Spain by Isabelle Darmon and colleagues; a comparison of credit-based systems of learning in London and Northern France by Pat Davies; a study of the links between initial and continuing education in Scotland, Northern Ireland and England by Tom Schuller and Andrew Burns; a comparison of policy strategies to reduce the divisions between academic and vocational learning in England and Scotland by David Raffe and colleagues; and, finally, reflections on devising and conducting cross-national studies in the social sciences by Antje Cockrill and colleagues.

[3] The third report, entitled *Speaking truth to power: Research and policy on lifelong learning*, contains two overview articles on the impact of research on policy (by Frank Coffield and Maurice Kogan); a chapter on the impact of the manager on learning in the workplace (by Michael Eraut, Jane Alderton, Gerald Cole and Peter Senker); a study of a post-compulsory education and training market in one urban locale in London (by Stephen Ball, Sheila Macrae and Meg Maguire); an examination of the policy implications of changes in training of NHS staff (by Therese Dowswell, Bobbie Millar and Jenny Hewison); the first findings from a major new survey of the skills of a representative sample of British workers (by Alan Felstead, David Ashton, Brendan Burchell and Francis Green); and, finally, a paper on the provision of adult guidance services in England (by Will Bartlett and Teresa Rees).

[4] The findings from *The Learning Society Programme* are available in two forms. A set of summaries in hard copy is available, free of charge, from Frank Coffield, Department of Education, University of Newcastle, St Thomas' Street, Newcastle upon Tyne, NE1 7RU. The same summaries are also available from the programme's website, whose address is http://www.staff.ncl.ac.uk/f.j.coffield/. It also provides more detailed information on publications by individual projects as well as by the programme as a whole.

[5] See, for instance, the claim made in the government's White Paper, *Learning to succeed*: "In the information and knowledge based economy, investment in human capital – in the intellect and creativity of people – is replacing past patterns of investment in plant, machinery and physical labour" (DfEE, 1999, p 12). For a detailed critique of this approach, see Coffield (1999).

[6] Researchers within the programme are currently producing the first comprehensive and critical treatment of social capital. See Baron et al, forthcoming.

[7] I wish to express my grateful thanks to Tony Edwards, the most friendly of critics and the least critical of friends, for his comments on an earlier draft of this paper.

References

Alheit, P. (1999) 'On a contradictory way to the Learning Society: a critical approach', *Studies in the Education of Adults*, vol 31, no 1, pp 66-82.

Ball, S., Maguire, M. and Macrae, S. (1999) 'Whose Learning Society? The post-16 education and training market in one urban locale', ESRC Conference on The Learning Society, London, 6 July.

Baron, S., Field, J. and Schuller, T. (eds) (forthcoming) *Social capital: Critical perspectives*, Oxford: Oxford University Press.

Bentley, T. (1998) *Learning beyond the classroom: Education for a changing world*, London: Routledge.

Bourdieu, P. (1977) 'Cultural reproduction and social reproduction', in J. Karabel and A.H. Halsey (eds) *Power and ideology in education*, New York, NY: Oxford University Press, pp 487-511.

Brown, A. and Keep, E. (forthcoming) *Review of vocational education and training research in the United Kingdom*, Luxembourg: European Commission.

CBI (Confederation of British Industries) (1989) *Towards a skills revolution*, London: CBI.

CBI (1991) *World class targets*, London: CBI.

CBI (1995) *Realising the vision: A skills passport*, London: CBI.

Coffield, F. (ed) (1997) *A national strategy for lifelong learning*, Newcastle: Department of Education, University of Newcastle.

Coffield, F. (1999) *Breaking the consensus: Lifelong learning as social control*, Inaugural Lecture, Department of Education, University of Newcastle, 2 February.

DfEE (Department for Education and Employment) (1997) *The Learning Age: A renaissance for a new Britain*, Cm 3790, London: The Stationery Office.

DfEE (1999) *Learning to succeed: A new framework for post-16 learning*, Cm 4392, London: The Stationery Office.

Dowswell, T., Millar, S. and Hewison, J. (1999) 'The costs of learning: the policy implications of changes in continuing education for NHS staff', in F. Coffield (ed) *Speaking truth to power: Research and policy on lifelong learning*, Bristol: The Policy Press.

Edwards, T. (1997) 'Contrasts in learning?', in T. Edwards, C.T. Fitz-Gibbon, F. Hardman, R. Haywood and N. Meagher (eds) *Separate but equal? A levels and GNVQs*, London: Routledge.

Eraut, M. (1997) 'Perspectives on defining "The Learning Society"', *Journal of Education Policy*, vol 12, no 6, November-December, pp 551-8.

Eraut, M. (1999) 'Learning in the workplace', in *Findings from the Learning Society Programme*, Newcastle: Department of Education, University of Newcastle.

Felstead, A., Ashton, D., Burchell, B. and Green, F. (1999) 'Skill trends in Britain: trajectories over the last decade', in F. Coffield (ed) *Speaking truth to power: Research and policy on lifelong learning*, Bristol: The Policy Press, pp 55-72.

Kumar, K. (1997) 'The need for place', in A. Smith and F. Webster (eds) *The postmodern university? Contested visions of higher education in society*, Buckingham: Open University Press and Society for Research into Higher Education, pp 27-35.

Lave, J. and Wenger, E. (1991) *Situated learning: Legitimate peripheral participation*, Cambridge and New York, NY: Cambridge University Press.

McGivney, V. (1999) *Informal learning in the community: A trigger for change and development*, Leicester: NIACE.

NIACE (National Institute for Adult and Continuing Education) (1999) *Briefing on the government White Paper, Learning to succeed*, Leicester: NIACE.

Pahl, R.E. (1991) 'The search for social cohesion: from Durkheim to the European Commission', *European Journal of Sociology*, vol 32, pp 345-60.

Tough, A. (1979) *The adult's learning projects: A fresh approach to theory and practice in adult education*, Toronto: OISE Press.

Young, M.F.D. (1998) *The curriculum of the future*, London: Falmer Press.

Non-formal learning, implicit learning and tacit knowledge in professional work

Michael Eraut

Towards a typology of non-formal learning

Informal learning is often treated as a residual category to describe any type of learning which does not take place within, or follow from, a formally organised learning programme or event. However, for those of us who believe that the majority of human learning does not occur in formal contexts, the utility of such a catch-all label is not very great. The term 'informal' is associated with so many other features of a situation – such as dress, discourse, behaviour, diminution of social differences – that its colloquial application as a descriptor of learning contexts may have little to do with learning per se. To avoid such confusion, the term 'non-formal learning' is preferable as the contrast to formal learning, and to make further distinctions within that heading.

The following characteristics of a learning situation can be defined as falling into the category of formal learning:

- a prescribed learning framework;
- an organised learning event or package;
- the presence of a designated teacher or trainer;
- the award of a qualification or credit;
- the external specification of outcomes.

However, in making this distinction it is important to avoid giving formal learning a negative connotation by embarking on an ill-informed critique such as Knowles' (1970) attack on pedagogy. Another proviso is that although learning of some type is always going on, because that is a

fundamental characteristic of human beings, this chapter is not concerned with learning of only momentary significance. Its focus is on non-formal learning that either contributes to "significant changes in capability or understanding" (Eraut, 1997) or is associated with non-routine aspects of a new task or encounter. In a wide-ranging chapter of this type, the precise meaning of the term 'learning' will vary a little with the context.

This chapter will explore the range of learning modes within the domain of *non-formal learning*, for which a simple typology is proposed. The most fundamental distinction is the level of intention to learn. At one extreme there is the now widely recognised phenomenon of implicit learning, at the other there is *deliberative learning* in time specifically set aside for that purpose. Reber (1993) defined *implicit learning* as "the acquisition of knowledge independently of conscious attempts to learn and in the absence of explicit knowledge about what was learned": there is no intention to learn and no awareness of learning at the time it takes place. It is useful to introduce one further category here, that of *reactive learning*. This lies between implicit learning and deliberative learning and is used to describe situations where the learning is explicit but takes place almost spontaneously in response to recent, current or imminent situations without any time being specifically set aside for it. Reactive learning is near-spontaneous and unplanned, the learner is aware of it but the level of intentionality will vary and will often be debatable. Its articulation in explicit form could also be difficult without setting aside time for more reflection and thus becoming deliberative.

The other dimension of non-formal learning which is useful in mapping this domain concerns the timing of the events that provide the focus for the learning. Are they events from the past, something happening in the present or part of some possible future action? The dimensions *time of local event* and *level of intention* can be combined to construct a simple typology of non-formal learning (Table 1).

The term 'self-directed learning' has not been used because it applies equally to formal and non-formal contexts: it is clearly deliberative rather than reactive and its advocates use it for that very reason (Long et al, 1996; Straka, 1997).

The version of *reflection* used by Dewey (1933) and Kolb (1984) is also deliberative and classified under *review* in the typology given in Table 1: Schön (1983) would describe it as 'reflection-*on*-action'. Schön's contrasting term 'reflection-*in*-action' is more problematic because it could be construed either as a reactive learning response to an event in the immediate past or as referring to a metacognitive awareness that triggers learning or decision making but is not in itself a form of learning (Eraut, 1995). Marsick's and Watkins' (1990) definition of *incidental learning* includes implicit learning, whereas the one put forward in this chapter does not. Planned non-formal learning is clearly deliberative, but so also is the learning that forms an integral part of deliberative activities such as decision making, planning and problem solving. 'Emergent' is the term used by Megginson (1996) to describe an alternative strategy to planning; but using an emergent strategy for defining goals need not prevent a deliberative rather than reactive approach when learning opportunities occur.

Implicit learning and tacit knowledge

The effects of implicit learning on future behaviour are well documented by Berry (1997), Reber (1993) and Underwood (1996). However, these effects could not have occurred unless some selection of lived experience had previously entered long-term memory, albeit not as part of a conscious, deliberate process. The reference to linkage with past memories is there because the effects can only be explained as resulting from the accumulated experience of several episodes rather than from a single event. However, there is no conscious awareness of the memories of these episodes having been combined to form a tacit knowledge base which enables future action.

Horvath et al (1996) explain both implicit learning and tacit knowledge, the outcome of such learning, in terms of Tulving's (1972) theory of memory. This distinguishes between episodic memory for specific, personally experienced events and semantic memory for generalised knowledge that transcends particular episodes. Researchers have been particularly interested in the traffic between the two. "According to models of inductive learning (eg, Holland) the transition from event knowledge to generalised knowledge involves mental processes that are sensitive to the covariance structure of the

Table 1: A typology of non-formal learning

Time of stimulus	Implicit learning	Reactive learning	Deliberative learning
Past episode(s)	Implicit linkage of past memories with current experience	Brief **near-spontaneous reflection** on past episodes, communications, events, experiences	**Review** of past actions, communications, events, experiences. More systematic reflection
Current experience	A selection from experience enters the memory	**Incidental** noting of facts, opinions, impressions, ideas **Recognition of** learning opportunities	**Engagement** in decision making, problem solving, planned informal learning
Future behaviour	Unconscious effect of previous experiences	Being prepared for **emergent** learning opportunities	**Planned** learning goals. **Planned** learning opportunities

Figure 1: Memory structures and knowledge-acquisition pathways in the explanatory model of tacit knowledge

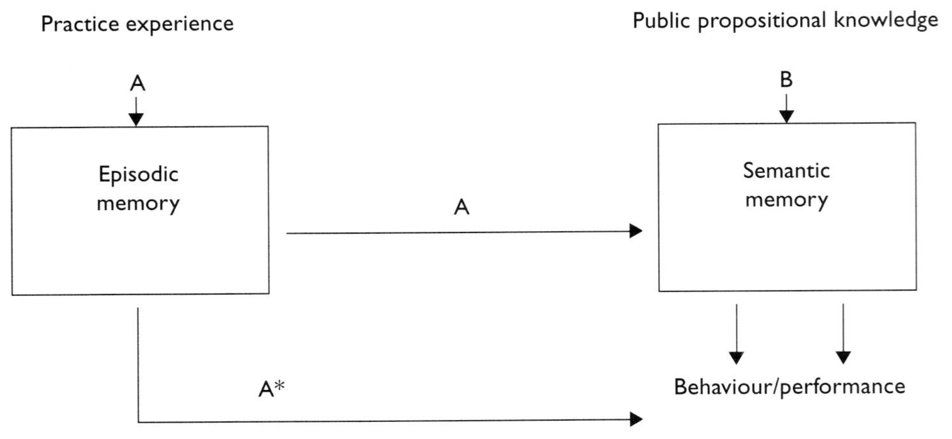

Source: Modified from Hovarth et al (1996)

environment, to 'what goes with what' in the world" (Horvarth et al, 1996, p 7). These processes of induction or abstraction isolate shared features and/or structures across episodes and "construct abstract or general representations of that shared structure" (Horvarth et al, 1996, p 7). The examples they quote suggest that they associate semantic memory primarily with propositional forms of generalised knowledge.

Figure 1 presents a diagrammatic representation of this theory. The top of the figure represents the sources of inputs to the memory system and the bottom of the figure represents the behavioural consequences of learning (the output of the memory system); the arrow between the boxes depicts the processes whereby generalised knowledge is derived from episodic memory. Path A in the diagram corresponds to what Kolb (1984) defines as experiential learning, whereby "personally experienced events are stored in episodic memory and, over time, used to construct generalised knowledge structures in semantic memory" (p 8). Path B depicts the direct acquisition of generalisable knowledge from other people. Path A* depicts implicit learning, described by Horvath et al as "the direct influence of event knowledge in episodic memory on behaviour – influence that is not mediated by the generalised knowledge representations in semantic memory" (1996, p 8). The existence of tacit knowledge acquired by Path A* is inferred from the nature of the observed behaviour.

In practice, multiple pathways are likely to be in use. The same episodes may contribute to performance both implicitly via Path A* and explicitly via Path A. For example, an encounter with a new situation fairly similar to some of those previously experienced may lead to rapid recognition via Path A* and generation of a previously used decision option (also via Path A*), possibly with an awareness that the match between the two situations might not be good enough for a repeat to be the best action. Explicit checking out of the option may then follow using generalised knowledge created by Path A. Another possibility is that knowledge acquired by both Path A and Path B is combined. Path B knowledge is often useful in reflecting on and clarifying the meaning of experienced events or in fitting new Path A knowledge into a broader conceptual structure (an important aim of formal mid-career courses). Conversely, Path A knowledge (and probably also Path A* knowledge) is helpful, perhaps essential, for learning how to use Path B knowledge in practical situations. Typically, tacit Path A* knowledge is ready to use while Path B knowledge is too abstract to be used without considerable further learning. So if a situation demands rapid action or is too complex to be analysed fully, tacit knowledge is the only available solution. These issues will be revisited later on in this chapter, but it is important from the outset to recognise that tacit knowledge is not a sideshow but central to important, everyday action.

Investigating non-formal learning

The problems faced by researchers investigating non-formal learning are considerable. Not only is implicit learning difficult to detect without prolonged observation, but reactive learning and some deliberative learning are unlikely to be consciously recalled unless there was an unusually dramatic outcome. Worse still, potential respondents are unaccustomed to talking about learning and may find it difficult to respond to a request to do so. If they do, they are more likely to refer to formal learning rather than non-formal learning. The latter is just part of their work: solving a problem at work is unlikely to be interpreted as a learning process unless an interviewer can home in on it in a particularly appropriate way. Given all these difficulties the study of the *Development of knowledge and skills in employment* made by Eraut et al (1998) was planned with the work of other previous researchers in mind.

The McCall et al (1988) study of 191 successful executives from six major US companies investigated how they learned from experience by asking them to talk about at least three key events or episodes in their career that led to a lasting change in their approach to management. In comparison with this focus on 'lifetime high points', the leading question in the Fox et al (1989) study of 356 physicians in North America was a little more modest: 'What changes have you made or have occurred in your life or practice during the past year?' An average of 22 changes was reported for that year, although many had earlier antecedents. The researchers' follow-up questions were 'What caused the change to occur?' and 'Did you learn anything in order to make this change?' Both of these studies yielded valuable findings, which shall be referred to later rather than now so as not to confine our attention to just the more salient learning episodes.

Gear et al's (1994) British inquiry was based on Tough's (1971) concept of a learning project, an extended piece of learning with a particular idea in mind. Their respondents were asked to select only one such project for discussion, but half of them had carried out between two and five more projects in the previous three years. Although this focus might seem likely to emphasise the planned aspect of

professional learning, less than one fifth claimed to have unequivocally followed a pre-determined plan. Out of the group, 80% had an idea of the outcome they wanted but followed an emergent strategy which took advantage of learning opportunities as they arose – the intent and the learning activity were deliberative, but the recognition of learning opportunities was reactive.

Mumford et al's (undated) study of 144 directors in 41 organisations used an approach even closer to the study by myself and my colleagues (Eraut et al, 1998a). They asked their respondents first about the skills they felt were necessary for their role, then about the processes and experiences which had led to their development. They started as we did, with a description of the work itself, but excluded knowledge and understanding from the discussion. Presumably they were not aware of recent research on decision making (Klein, et al 1993), a critically important aspect of the senior manager's role.

Given our concern to include the learning that is needed for, and arises from, taken-for-granted aspects of daily work, we returned to the questioning strategy, used by two of us in earlier research on the use of scientific knowledge by nurses and midwives (Eraut et al, 1995). This was adapted to focus on learning rather than knowledge use and promised to elicit a wider range of learning experiences than those 'captured' by the projects discussed above.

Our strategy for the first interviews was to:

- ask about the nature of the respondent's job, recent tasks, duties and problems;

- discuss the nature of the competence/expertise required to do it;

- ask how the necessary expertise was acquired and the extent to which it was changing;

- ask about different sources of learning, if these had not already become apparent.

Respondents were also encouraged to elaborate on salient learning episodes or to exemplify general statements about learning. Most of the interviews lasted between one and two hours, and many of those interviewed stated that they had found it a valuable experience which had stimulated their thinking about learning. The first interviews often yielded some evidence on the factors affecting learning, although we did not intend to introduce that question until our second interviews.

These first interviews were transcribed and provisionally analysed by the interviewer, then converted into interim reports on each occupational sector for discussion at a meeting with representatives of the 12 engineering, business and healthcare organisations where we did our research. This discussion raised a number of questions to be addressed by further analysis, and was followed by a brainstorming session on categories to be included in our framework for analysing the data. These were then classified, checked for consistency and elaborated in certain areas to take account of other research findings. The draft framework was then sent to our contacts with a report of the meeting and used for further analysis of our interview transcripts. During this further analysis researchers also noted points needing elaboration in the second interview, and categories where the absence or paucity of information needed to be checked in case it had been an artefact of the interview situation. Transcripts were sent to respondents about a month before their second interview, with a request for suggested modifications and a list of questions arising from the first interview. Thus second interviews focused partly on elaboration of the first and partly on our third research question about factors affecting the amount and direction of their learning. Those who gave the richest first interviews usually gave equally rich second interviews, suggesting greater self-awareness in the area of learning. The framework was then further revised and became a valuable outcome from our research.

Both before and during our fieldwork we were acutely aware of the difficulty of getting respondents not only to describe their job when many aspects of it were likely to be taken for granted, but also to progress from that description to discuss the nature of the competence and expertise which enabled them to do that job. They were aware that they had learned implicitly to do many things which formed part of their job, but they could not easily describe their personal knowledge and know-how. The interesting theoretical question, which also has many practical consequences, is whether this knowledge was capable of being elicited by the right questions and opportunities for respondents to think about those questions, or whether it was indeed tacit knowledge which they were not able to talk to us about.

Definition and elicitation of tacit knowledge

Like 'informal learning', the term tacit knowledge has acquired a wide range of meanings. On the one hand Polanyi (1967) defined it as "that which we know but cannot tell", while on the other a whole string of authors talk about making tacit knowledge explicit: this can mean either that the knower learns to tell or that the researcher tells and then seeks respondent verification. There are two aspects of this problem: awareness and representation. A person may be socialised into the norms of an organisation without being aware either of the learning or of what some of the norms are. Besides being an example of implicit learning, it is possible to imagine many types of event which might trigger awareness of these norms, for example, transgressions by a third party might cause negative responses which then need to be explained. Sometimes, there is no problem in the 'telling' once awareness has been established: implicit learning may eventually lead to explicit knowledge. However, the opposite can also be true, explicit learning can lead to tacit knowledge. For example, a person may be very aware of being able to ride a bicycle and able to describe how they learned to do it, without being able to describe critical aspects of the knowledge gained, such as rapid responses to a sense of impending imbalance, while other relevant knowledge, such as the steadying effect of the gyroscopic motion of the wheels, would almost certainly never be acquired. No doubt a physicist could compile a video of someone finally achieving competence and provide a commentary, but it would be difficult to claim that this represented the knowledge of the average cyclist.

Given the awareness that one possesses certain knowledge, there are many possible ways that people may describe tacit knowledge, ranging from a glimpse, through an insight or perspective to what many might regard as a reasonable, though not complete, representation of the whole. One major difficulty is presented by the medium, another by the genre(s) in which 'acceptable' descriptions have to be communicated. For example, when researchers talk about making tacit knowledge explicit they often imply that this means presenting it as a set of propositions, like the findings from a piece of research. Most authors using the term tacit knowledge tend to treat it as a catch-all category, without seeking to define it any further. Does it refer to knowledge which is not communicated, or knowledge which cannot be communicated? Is it an attribute of the knower, some can communicate it, some cannot; or is it an attribute of the knowledge itself? Could it be an element of both? Researchers are acutely aware that some people 'tell more' than others who perform at a similar level of competence; there is also evidence that some types of knowledge are easier to communicate than others. Can a skilful researcher communicate what their respondents cannot and does that suggest that the researcher is a good novelist, a potential poet or an expert in knowledge elicitation?

Spender (1995) focuses on epistemological status rather than communicability, suggesting that tacit knowledge be defined as "that which has not yet been abstracted from practice", thus linking it to Path A* in Figure 1. However, Molander (1992) argues that there is no knowledge which is totally tacit and none without at least some tacit aspect. The problem for researchers is to reach as far as they can down the continuum from explicit to tacit knowledge. In either case, there are two possible approaches to knowledge elicitation: to facilitate the 'telling' or to elucidate sufficient information to infer the nature of the knowledge being discussed. Both methods require the researcher to construct an account, and it is good practice to submit this account to respondents for verification or modification. The other conclusion to be drawn from Molander's argument is the warning that even the most complete, explicit account of expertise from an ideal witness will still lack aspects of tacit knowledge which remain unrecalled and undisclosed.

The strategy for facilitating the telling which we used in our research for *The Learning Society Programme* has already been described. Although this helped us to extend previous research and to construct a more comprehensive picture of learning at work, we also became aware of the limitations of

an interview-based approach. This was partly due to the width of our domain, and partly to the limitations of single or even double interviews for eliciting evidence of processes that, if not entirely tacit, do not readily come to mind. A prolonged period of fieldwork, perhaps two weeks in each participant's workplace, would have enabled us to gather much more evidence about workplace activities, decisions and transactions; this would then have prompted many more questions about the learning which made their performance possible. Nevertheless, we were able to reflect on factors other than individual characteristics which affected how much respondents seemed able to tell us, even within the limitations of our particular project.

These factors affecting the capability to tell were linked to people's prior experiences of talking about what they knew. Talking more explicitly about their knowledge at work was more likely to occur when there was one of the following situations in place:

- some mediating object such as a picture or a drawing which colleagues were accustomed to discussing, eg an x-ray image, a video, a diagrammatic representation of a piece of equipment, a graph or a set of figures;

- a climate of regular mutual consultation encouraging those consulted to describe what they know;

- a training or mentoring relationship in which explanations were expected, sometimes of cultural or behavioural norms as well as more technical matters;

- an informal relationship leading to work-related discussions of information out of hours, when more 'provisional' and 'riskier' comments might be made which conveyed some meaning but were not understood as pretending to be comprehensive or accurate;

- a crisis, review or radical change in practice, which caused people to exchange opinions and experiences, sometimes with the outcome that values were made more explicit.

Another factor was the role of continuing education in the form of courses or serious reading. For many respondents this added an important dimension to their ability to think and talk about their work situation when it provided a vocabulary for talking about aspects of their experiences which had been previously difficult to discuss and concepts and theories which helped them to make sense of their experience and understand issues and alternative perspectives more clearly. This was particularly true of mid-career courses which build on participants' experiences, the most frequently cited examples being in management. For example, studying organisational behaviour helped our respondents to comprehend aspects of their own context of which they were partially aware but had not previously understood; studying the management of change helped them to understand why so many new initiatives had failed to be fully implemented and ground to a halt. Many people were helped to move their thinking from a purely organisational level to a strategic level and/or to see their organisation's relationship with its environment from a different perspective. The net effect was an enhanced capacity and greater confidence to think and talk about their own work and its organisational context. Such educational experiences were not simply making tacit knowledge explicit, but using some of their tacit knowledge as one component of a more developed, as well as more explicit, understanding of their working situation. These positive experiences of mid-career education were not reported by the majority of our respondents, many of whom lacked such opportunities; but they have been confirmed by other research on the learning outcomes of management courses (Webber, 1999).

The other approach which can aid the communication of knowledge depends on the researchers' ability to suggest types of knowledge that might be in use in a particular situation and to get the respondent to confirm, modify or deny their suggestions. To achieve this researchers need a repertoire of types of knowledge and knowledge use and the ability to gain sufficient understanding of their respondent's situation and to develop ideas from that repertoire in a manner that is both appropriate to the situation and meaningful to their respondent. They also have to be able to develop relationships that empower their respondents to be brutally honest about what they think of the researcher's suggestions and to give the respondents the opportunity for a second, more considered response. More situationally-located styles of interviewing and researcher-initiated suggestions need to be pursued, but modestly and reflexively,

with the underpinning awareness that there will always be multiple representations of the knowledge embedded in any complex situation.

Tacit knowledge of people and contexts

The next two sections of this chapter explore the range of contexts in which tacit knowledge is likely to be found. The first is primarily about tacit understanding, the second is about tacit knowledge in action. One of the most important features of any workplace or community context is the people with whom you interact – colleagues, friends, customers, clients, acquaintances. Yet much knowledge of other people is tacit: although you might gossip about them, you do not often have to put knowledge of people into words unless it is a specific part of your job, and you might find it difficult to do so. Yet such knowledge provides the basis of unhesitating daily interactions with others. It appears to fit the Horvath et al (1996) model quite well. Knowledge of another person is mainly gathered from a series of encounters set up for other purposes: only a small percentage of meetings will have getting to know that person as an objective, most often it is an incidental side effect. Yet in order to respond, you have to assume some knowledge of the person you are talking with and this will be based on accumulated knowledge from previous encounters which you neither make explicit nor question. Such knowledge is unlikely to be under your critical control. You may also have explicit knowledge of that person created through reflection or gathered from other sources, but it is unlikely to replace the tacit knowledge which enables you to respond instantly to people you know. Such knowledge is part of your taken-for-granted understanding of that person, and is liable to be both biased and self-confirming.

Reasons for tacit knowledge of other people being biased include the fact that:

- our series of encounters with another person are unlikely to provide a typical sample of his or her behaviour: the reasons and circumstances for the meetings will largely determine the nature of those encounters, and our own presence is also likely to affect what happens;

- we are most likely to remember events within those encounters that demand our attention, that is, those that are most 'memorable' rather than those that are most common;
- preconceptions, created by earlier encounters, affect both parties' behaviour on later occasions, so the sample is not constructed from genuinely independent events;
- people develop personal constructs (Kelly, 1955), or ways of construing their environment, as a result of their life experiences and these affect their understanding of, and hence behaviour towards, those whom they meet.

People are predisposed to interpret other people's actions in particular ways, creating preconceptions at early encounters that determine their own behaviour. This will affect how others respond to them which will often be in ways that will tend to confirm those preconceptions. While tacit knowledge of other people will continue to play an important part in our lives because it is available for almost instant use whenever we need it, it will rarely be as valid and unbiased as we like to assume. Greater self-awareness and remedial action will often be required (Eraut, 1994).

Knowledge of contexts and organisations is often acquired through a process of socialisation through observation, induction and increasing participation rather than formal inquiry. Norms, local discourse and other aspects of an organisational or occupational culture are acquired over a significant period of time by processes which implicitly add meaning to what are explicitly interpreted as routine activities. For example, Tomlinson (1999) points out that as a result of many years of schooling, student teachers implicitly 'know what teachers do'. Even though they may explicitly argue, and have personally experienced, that many teaching activities do not promote learning, this may be overridden by their implicit knowledge of teachers when they are confronted by a combination of the practical need to take charge of a classroom and the psychological need to be identified as a genuine teacher and not just a student. Implicit knowledge can be very powerful indeed even when, as in most teacher training, explicit knowledge is available in plenty.

Particularly frustrating for the researcher is the possibility that language itself may serve purposes other than making knowledge or actions explicit. Learning to talk to clients or colleagues or managers may be at best a semiconscious process, during which the latent functions of the discourse are not revealed and may even remain hidden from the qualified professional participants. For example, the manifest function of discourse could be to consult and inform clients, to keep colleagues aware of your actions and to render an account of your actions to managers. The latent functions may be to keep clients happy while asserting the professional role, to maintain good relations with colleagues while preserving freedom from their influence, and to tell managers what they want to hear while keeping them off your back. To serve the manifest function will often require congruence between what is said and what is done; but this may constrain the latent function. Where discourse in some professional settings has evolved to serve such latent purposes, its use in other settings may impede rather than enhance understanding of practice. In general, discourse in many settings helps to provide a defensible account rather than a description of professionals' actions and to create an impression of professional control over situations which inspires confidence in them as persons. It may seek to disguise rather than share uncertainty and risk-taking. Technical vocabulary, labelling of clients or their problems, and in some cases the use of numerical data, all help to achieve these purposes. It is now common practice for researchers to recognise that explicit accounts do not provide 'the whole truth', but it is relatively rare outside the overtly political domain to suggest that such accounts may mislead because implicitly acquired discourse has developed for that very purpose.

Another feature of a person's understanding of people and organisations is what are commonly referred to as implicit theories: inferred correlations or causal linkages between attributes of a person or an organisation. These theories are called implicit, because they are seldom explicitly stated by the knower but used by psychologists to explain his or her behaviour. Those observed behave as if they believed the implicit theory imputed to them. The psychological explanation for the lack of explicitness is that such theories form part of the taken-for-granted world of the knower, their social reality.

The validity of this approach is confirmed both by the logic of the observations and by the recognition, albeit delayed, of implicit theories by their knowers in situations where there is no strong reason for them wishing to deny them. Horvath et al's (1996) paper quotes examples of such implicit theories, whose position in their model (Figure 1) is unclear. Path A is described as "constructing generalised knowledge structures in semantic memory", which amounts to a process by which tacit knowledge is made explicit. However, implicit theories appear to be a form of tacit knowledge stored in semantic memory in propositional form. Compared with other forms of tacit knowledge they can be readily made explicit by researchers and confirmed by their informants; but by remaining tacit they escape the influence of other, more explicit, public theories, acquired by Path B. The knowledge privacy of the implicit theorist provides protection from criticism.

Argyris and Schön (1974) provided another perspective on implicit theories when they made their classic distinction between espoused theories and theories in use. Their theories in use closely match the examples given by Horvath et al, being experientially developed and very close to being made explicit. However, the contrast with espoused theories which provide explicit explanations of their actions introduces yet another dimension to our discussion. According to Argyris and Schön the central problem for most managers and professionals is that they are intellectually and emotionally committed to espoused theories which describe the world as they would like it to be, but which do not accurately describe their own actions. The result is that they do not understand, indeed do not even perceive, the effects of their own actions. They tend to perceive (and in the case of managers be told by their subordinates) what they want or expect to perceive, thus receiving self-confirmation of their actions. This results in misperceiving 'what goes with what' and developing false experiential theories of action. The problem can only be solved, according to Argyris and Schön, by stepping outside their taken-for-granted world and espoused theories to search for genuine feedback on the outcomes of their actions: they called this double-loop learning to distinguish it from self-confirmatory single-loop learning.

Eraut (1994) has argued that the mismatch between espoused theories and theories in use is a natural consequence of the prevailing dualistic approach to professional education. Espoused theories are developed in education contexts and their comprehension rewarded by the assessment system. They also represent the way professions like to see themselves and present themselves to the public. Theories in use are developed quite separately to cope with the exigencies of practice and even if explicit would not 'be deemed fit for public communication' as they would diminish the image of the profession. Apart from preserving the often mourned but rarely narrowed theory–practice gap in many professions, espoused theories provide professionals with a 'professional conscience' which urges them to judge their work according to a form of idealised practice which is unachievable. Over time this leads either to scepticism or to frustration and burnout or they become professional educators and perpetuate the cycle. The domain of explicit and implicit theories of action is complex and little understood but also highly significant.

Tacit knowledge in action

Action is described as routinised when actors no longer need to think about what they are doing because they have done it so many times before. Routinisation starts by following other people, or manuals or checklists or even self-devised procedures: these may be simple sequences with only one pathway or algorithm whose pathways diverge as you proceed. Learning by repetition enables the actor first to reach the stage where the aid of a person or checklist is no longer required and then to progress to a future stage where an internalised explicit description of the procedure also becomes redundant and eventually falls into disuse. Routinisation can apply not only to simple procedures such as changing gear when driving a car but also to complex skills such as reading. However, even the most fluent readers may be momentarily halted by an unfamiliar word or a clumsy clause structure. In effect, reading complex material involves implicit routinised behaviour punctuated by short bursts of explicit attention to the words themselves rather than the meaning they convey. This is typical of skilled behaviour, though sometimes the interruption comes from the context rather than the task itself. One of the most frequently cited examples of tacit knowledge, riding a bicycle, becomes far from routine when surrounded by heavy traffic. In addition to the basic routine of riding along and keeping your balance there is a succession of reflex actions and rapid decisions caused by the traffic; there may also be some more deliberative thinking about the route to take especially if the avoidance of traffic is a possible option. The picture is not dissimilar to that portrayed by Jackson (1971) when he suggested that a primary school teacher makes a thousand decisions a day.

Two apparently opposite processes have now been identified: experiential learning (if you follow the Kolb model) involves deriving explicit knowledge through reflection on experiences which might otherwise remain in episodic memory and be used only tacitly; routinisation involves explicit procedural knowledge being converted to tacit knowledge through repetition. However, neither can be found in their pure form. Routines are regularly interrupted by short periods of problem solving to resolve difficulties or decision making to adapt to changes in the external context. Experience cannot be represented only by abstract propositions. Horvath et al (1996) infer from their interviews of military commanders a set of 'tacit knowledge' propositions about leadership. While they state that it would be pointless to try and teach these propositions to trainees who lack the requisite experience they do not explain their reasons. One interpretation of this is that they have impaled themselves on a proposition-based definition of tacit knowledge. However, these propositions, like other maxims, do not represent the full range of knowledge in use; they may be little more than *aides-mémoire*. Most of the tacit knowledge lies in recognising the situation as one in which the maxim is appropriate – what Klein (1989) calls "recognition primed decision making". Although such maxims may not have played any part in previous actions, making them explicit may help to draw attention to the context and conditions where it is appropriate to use them. That is when the 'real' tacit knowledge begins to be disclosed and further learning is more likely to occur.

It is now appropriate to examine the polar opposite of tacit knowledge, classical decision theory. This involves constructing mathematical models of decision-making situations so that calculation can be used to determine the relative merits of different options. These models are not dealing with certainties – they rarely occur – but with probabilities. Since there is good evidence that naturalistic judgement gets complex situations involving combinations of probabilities badly wrong, the approach is not without its use. It can also take into account the respective values that people attach to different options. However, to be useful there must be a sufficiently good match between the model and the decision making situation being modelled and sufficiently good 'probability for outcome' data and 'utility' data (utility is the technical term for the value attached to a particular outcome).

This theory gave rise to applications in business and medicine as well as the continuing development of economics. A pioneering book by Weinstein and Fineberg (1980) led to the approach we now call evidence-based medicine. This incorporates both a research and policy strand and a practitioner's strand. The research strand emphasises meta-analyses of research studies with priority being accorded to those involving randomised control trials. Current British policy is focused on using both research and expert meetings to compile practice guidelines which are graded at three levels, those based on:

- control trials alone;
- a wider selection of research evidence;
- agreements by experts in areas where there is insufficient research evidence for level 1 or 2 reports.

There is also a fourth type of situation, where the amount of evidence and expert agreement is too small to be able to produce any defensible set of guidelines. This attempt to map the corpus of explicit medical knowledge is bringing out both the strengths and limitations of what Schön (1983) calls the technical–rationality paradigm. In some areas the focus on research is saving many lives, in others the production of research-based guidelines is a distant aspiration. While the government rightly seeks to expand the research base into areas of greater complexity and uncertainty, not more than 20% of medical decisions are currently covered by existing or planned level 1 guidelines (this figure has been elicited from interviews with several people working in this area, although there is considerable disagreement over what it will be in 10 years' time). Responsibility for the remaining decisions reverts from national guidelines to less reliable guidelines or the unguided decisions of the individual practitioner or healthcare team.

How then are individual and/or team decisions made in the absence of research-based guidelines and what is the role in such decisions of tacit knowledge? Eraut (1999) has approached this issue by distinguishing between three modes of cognition – analytic, intuitive and deliberative – and discussing the factors that affect their relative importance in different situations. The analytic mode has two ideal types, evidence-based practice and theory-based argument. From a practitioner viewpoint evidence-based practice is not confined to following policy guidelines where they exist; it incorporates a general attitude towards evidence, and it seeks both to maximise the amount of evidence from systematic observation and recording and to interpret it more critically than is currently the norm (McMaster University, EBMWG, 1992). The McMaster group specifically warned that:

In the absence of systematic observation one must be cautious in the interpretation of information derived from clinical experience and intuition, for it may at times be misleading. (McMaster University, EBMWG, 1992, p 2421)

However, they also argue that "clinicians must be ready to accept and live with uncertainty and to acknowledge that management decisions are often made in the face of relative ignorance of their true impact" (McMaster University, EBMWG, 1992, p 2421).

There is a danger that the continuing discovery of the importance of tacit knowledge will lead some people to argue on ideological grounds that it should replace evidence-based practice. However, it is surely more reasonable to argue that we should seek to expand evidence-based practice but not suffer from any delusions about how far it will take us nor lose awareness of just how much interpretation of guidelines may be needed when making decisions about individual cases.

The difficulty of interpretation is even greater when considering the other analytic ideal type – the use of theory. Even in well-theorised areas of practice, the interpretation of theory is problematic and requires further learning from experience. For practitioners additional knowledge is required beyond the set of propositions taught as theory and the evidence suggests that this additional knowledge is highly situated and very often tacit (Eraut, 1999).

The intuitive mode of cognition relies more on prior experience than theory or research, and makes considerable use of tacit knowledge. Even when that knowledge is capable of being explicitly described by the actor, it may be used tacitly because that is usually quicker. The various aspects of the intuitive mode are conveniently introduced through the Skill Acquisition Model of Dreyfus and Dreyfus (1986), which brings together situational understanding, routinised action and decision making. They describe their model, which was originally developed to counter what they considered to be the overambitious claims of decision analysis, as an integrative overarching approach to professional action. Their model, presented in Table 2 opposite, depicts progression through five levels, from Novice to Expert.

Its early and middle stages involve: the development of situational recognition and understanding and of standard routines which enable the person to cope with crowded, busy contexts; the later abandonment of explicit rules and guidelines as behaviour becomes more automatic; a peaking of the deliberative mode of cognition (not usually very analytic) at the competence stage. Progression beyond competence is then associated with the gradual replacement of deliberation by more intuitive forms of cognition.

Tacit knowledge appears in their model in three different forms: as tacit understanding, tacit procedures and tacit rules:

- situational understanding is being developed through all five stages, based largely on experience and remaining mainly tacit;
- standard, routinised procedures are developed through to the competence stage for coping with the demands of work without suffering from information overload; some of them are likely to

Table 2: Summary of the Dreyfus skill acquisition model

Level 1   Novice
Rigid adherence to taught rules or plans
Little situational perception
No discretionary judgement

Level 2   Advanced beginner
Guidelines for action based on attributes
  or aspects (aspects are global
  characteristics of situations recognisable
  only after some prior experience)
Situational perception still limited
All attributes and aspects are treated
  separately and given equal importance

Level 3   Competent
Ability to cope with crowded, busy
  contexts
Now sees actions at least partially in terms
  of longer-term goals
Conscious deliberate planning
Uses standardised and routinised
  procedures

Level 4   Proficient
Sees situations holistically rather than in
  terms of aspects
Sees what is most important in a situation
Perceives deviations from the normal
  pattern
Decision making less laboured
Uses maxims for guidance, whose meaning
  varies according to the situation

Level 5   Expert
No longer relies on rules, guidelines or
  maxims
Has an intuitive grasp of situations based
  on deep tacit understanding
Only uses analytic approaches in novel
  situations, when problems occur or when
  justifying conclusions
Has a vision of what is possible

Source: From Eraut (1994)

have begun as explicit procedural knowledge then become automised and increasingly tacit through repetition, with concomitant increases in speed and productivity;

- increasingly intuitive decision making, in which not only pattern recognition but also rapid responses to developing situations are based on the tacit application of tacit rules; these rules may or may not be explicit or capable of reasoned justification, but their distinctive feature is that of being tacit at the moment of use.

Both Dreyfus and Dreyfus (1986) and Benner (1984) cite evidence to support the widespread use of rapid intuitive decision making by experts, but do not establish their claim that deliberation has become virtually redundant. Benner recognises two situations where analytic approaches might be required: when an expert is confronted with a situation of which he/she has no previous experience or when the expert gets a wrong grasp of a situation then finds that events and behaviours are not occurring as expected. Dreyfus and Dreyfus suggest yet a third possibility, that "detached deliberation about the validity of decisions will improve decision-making" (1986, p 164). Roughly translated, their advice is that if an intuitively derived decision proposal does not feel right or has an equally compelling alternative, think it through and check it out.

'Not feeling right' is an example of implicit monitoring, a meta-cognitive process which may trigger either immediate action or reflection followed by rapid action. The latter would correspond to what Schön (1983) calls "reflection-in-action", although Eraut (1995) points out that Schön's use of this term is inconsistent and its epistemological status uncertain.

The deliberative mode of cognition was first identified by Aristotle but is still difficult to define. Practitioners will usually be in deliberative mode when they are planning, evaluating, problem solving or reflecting on their experience. Some group discussions might be classed as group deliberations, and individual deliberations could often be described as discussions with oneself. Deliberation is similar to the intuitive mode in making considerable use of personal experience and similar to the analytic mode in being a mainly explicit process. Two purposes for deliberation can be usefully distinguished, although they are sometimes combined in practice: reflective deliberation, which has been discussed in considerable depth by Dewey (1933), aims to make sense of and/or evaluate your experience, including what you have heard and read; however, prospective deliberation is directed towards a future course of action and includes decision making and resolving contentious issues.

It is difficult to decide the extent to which deliberation is a distinctive mode of cognition, a mixture of analysis and intuition, or a hybrid of the two. Intuitive incidents occur at many stages of a deliberative process: retrieval from memory, recognition of a pattern, the sudden emergence of a new idea, the sense that a particular course of action will work. Periods of analysis will also occur during deliberative periods which provide sufficient time to do so. However, the problems and issues are usually too complex and too uncertain to be handled in a purely analytic mode. The argument for treating deliberation as a distinct mode is that for much of the time the thinking is neither intuitive nor analytic. It may involve: turning things over in your mind, looking at the situation from different angles; trying to make sense of many viewpoints, many sources of information and many theoretical perspectives; searching for ways to frame the problem; trying to reconcile conflicting factors; developing a new approach; or exploring possible scenarios. Another confusing feature is the status accorded to the finished product of thinking rather than the process of achieving it. The distinctive genre of the scientific paper or scientific book demonstrates what Kaplan (1964) called reconstructed logic rather than an account of their creation. This paper may appear to be an analysis of the phenomena of implicit learning and tacit knowledge, but its production involved a great deal of deliberation.

Eraut (1994) suggests that typical features of deliberative processes are:

- some uncertainty about outcomes;
- guidance from theory that is only partially helpful;
- relevant but often insufficient contextual knowledge;
- pressure on the time available for deliberation;
- a strong tendency to follow accustomed patterns of thinking;
- an opportunity, perhaps a requirement, to consult or involve other people.

These processes cannot be accomplished by using procedural knowledge alone or following a manual. They require a unique combination of propositional knowledge, situational knowledge, professional experience and judgement. The tendency to use familiar schemata is crucial for quick action in relatively familiar situations, but can be a major handicap when the situation is radically different – an important argument for involving other people.

What factors are likely to affect the mode of cognition used by a particular practitioner in a particular context? An analytic approach depends on there being sufficient research evidence available in which the practitioner has confidence, the problem being capable of being represented in a form that enables it to be 'solved' mainly on the basis of that evidence, and the practitioner being willing and able to do the analysis and implement the results. An intuitive approach requires that the practitioner has considerable experience of similar situations. A deliberative approach works best when the practitioner has both some evidence and some relevant experience, a willingness to reflect and consult and a sense of what is possible under the circumstances. What is at issue is not the use of evidence, as Hammersley (1997) points out, but "the relative importance of different kinds of evidence".

However, the conditions for good practice are not always present. So evidence, complexity and the practitioner's capability and disposition are not the only factors affecting mode of cognition. Two very important variables derive from the context rather than the agent or the task. These are the time available and the crowdedness of the situation, in other words, the number of clients, activities, pieces of information and so on that are competing for the practitioner's attention. Table 3 depicts the effects of time on mode of cognition. This relationship is probably interactive: shortage of time forces people to adopt a more intuitive approach, while the intuitive routines developed by experience enable people to do things more quickly. Crowded contexts also force people to be more selective with their attention and to process their incoming information more rapidly. Under conditions of rapid interpretation and decision making, meta-processes are limited to implicit monitoring and short, reactive reflections. However, as more time becomes available, the role of meta-processes becomes more complex, expanding beyond self-awareness and monitoring to include the framing of problems, thinking about the deliberative process itself and how it is being handled, searching for relevant knowledge, introducing value considerations and so on.

Table 3: Interactions between time, mode of cognition and type of thought/action

Thought/action	Mode of cognition		
	Instant/reflex	*Rapid/intuitive*	*Deliberative/analytic*
Reading of the situation	Pattern recognition	Rapid interpretation	Review involving discussions and/or analysis
Decision making	Instant response	Intuitive	Deliberative with some analysis or discussion
Overt activity	Routinised action	Routines punctuated by rapid decisions	Planned actions with periodic progress reviews
Metacognitive processes	Situational awareness	Implicit monitoring Short, reactive reflections	Conscious monitoring of thought and activity. Self-management Evaluation

The example given earlier of riding a bicycle in traffic involves the simultaneous operation of two or more modes of cognition. Maintaining balance and steering are fully automated activities, while responding to traffic movements may entail both reflex responses to sudden events and rapid intuitive responses to anticipatory readings of a developing complication. When the traffic is relatively calm, it would not be unusual to engage in deliberative thinking about your route or actions to be taken after reaching your destination. Such multiple mode operation is particularly evident in teamwork. In 'hot action' teams, such as a surgical team, a group of musicians or a football team, mutual dependence is high and close coordination essential. Mutual awareness and reflex responses maintain coordination, while momentary lapses are remedied by rapid decisions which restore synchrony. Experienced performers have both a developed sense of what it feels like to be working in perfect harmony and the capacity developed through long practice in a particular team to reach that ideal state. There would usually have been deliberative planning and decision making prior to performance as well as practice in working together. In 'cool action' teams engaged in a project, a deliberative mode is the established normal state; but when people interact in a more animated way, sparking each other off or arguing, rapid responses are likely to occur which lead to new insights. Participation in discussion often involves deliberative thinking about the topic, rapid comprehension of what others are saying, and rapid decision making about when to speak and what type of contribution to make. In every case there appears to be more than

one mental process in action: some make considerable use of explicit knowledge, while others rely mainly on tacit knowledge. Although the processes are distinguishable from each other, they also interact in ways we rarely comprehend.

Individual knowledge or social knowledge?

Eraut (1997) defines 'personal knowledge' as the cognitive resources that a person brings to a situation which enables them to think and perform. This includes both implicit knowledge and tacit knowledge, public knowledge and private knowledge. But to what extent is it really personal? There are two strong arguments against regarding knowledge as solely individual in nature. The first comes from evidence that in some situations a person is unable to perform on their own, so individual knowledge is necessary but not sufficient. The most obvious example is the 'hot action' teams described in the previous section. Another is when activities are sustained in an organisation by many different people who do not form a team and do not necessarily act together. These activities usually persist despite changes of personnel, so can the knowledge that sustains them be regarded as purely personal? Distributed cognition is the term used to describe such phenomena, although its use has been most commonly applied to people working with computers whose programmed knowledge contributes to their performance. It is argued that the performance of a person interacting with a computer is dependent not only on the knowledge of the individual but also on that of those who designed the programme and indeed the computer itself. This theme is well developed from a number of perspectives by Salomon (1993).

The second argument against conceiving knowledge as solely individual is an extension of the concept of situated learning. This paper has been arguing that knowledge is shaped by the context(s) in which it is acquired and used. Learning is always situated in a particular context which comprises not only a location and a set of activities in which knowledge either contributes or is embedded, but also a set of social relations which give rise to those activities. This raises the important question of the extent to which any given piece of knowledge is individually or socially constructed within that context. One increasingly popular theoretical response is to define cognition as that which enables social processes to take place and cannot therefore reside in the head of any one individual. This is congruent with the concept of distributive cognition but depersonalises cognition even further. This position is no more helpful than the traditional psychological view which defines cognition as a purely individual phenomenon. Neither accounts for the full complexity of knowledge and learning in action.

A simple typology suggested by Spender (1998) (see Table 4) backs up this view. This recognises both individual and social modes of cognition and maps them against the explicit–implicit distinction which has dominated much of this chapter.

Table 4: Individual and social modes of cognition

	Individual	Social
Explicit	Conscious	Objectified Scientific
Implicit	Automatic Intuitive	Collective Cultural

At the beginning of this chapter 'formal learning' was defined in terms of characteristics of the learning situation. But how does this map on to real situations? There is good evidence of many types of learning occurring (or sometimes not occurring) simultaneously in the archetypal context

for formal learning, the school. Explicitly stated curriculum knowledge, with which formal learning is usually identified, is only one aspect of the process. Pupils are also learning: how to present work for assessment; how to participate in shared discussions; algorithms and schemas for reading and problem solving; a hidden curriculum of orderly, disciplined behaviour, working to deadlines and submission to authority; and a rich array of knowledge, beliefs, attitudes and behaviour from peer group interaction. Can these separately listed forms of learning be separated from each other in practice? It is difficult to imagine a formal learning context in which only explicit learning of explicit knowledge takes place. To focus only on the explicit learning of formally presented knowledge is to fail to recognise the complexity of learning even in well-ordered classrooms. The knowledge gained is constructed in a social context whose influence on what is learned, as well as how it is learned, cannot be denied.

Where then is the evidence for individual cognition, if explicit knowledge and implicit knowledge are both socially constructed and socially mediated? Even in formal settings, research has shown huge individual differences, both quantitative and qualitative, within communal learning arrangements. Some can be attributed to observed differences in classroom transactions involving individuals: individual students receive differentiated treatment from their teachers and their peers, learn to respond to different people in different ways, and accumulate different episodes in their long-term memory. Other differences in outcomes can be attributed to the differences in prior knowledge and disposition with which they enter their school or college. Individuals do not enter a given setting with identical cognitive resources, the setting rarely treats them in a completely uniform way, and their experience is somewhat differentiated. The time spent in that setting is an important variable and access to knowledge will depend on a person's level of participation.

A significant feature of a very traditional society is a limited number of lifetime pathways through a limited number of social settings, with consequent constraints on access to knowledge and the size of the potentially available knowledge base. However, in a post-Fordist modern society there is a large range of social settings, a greater variety of people within those settings and a huge number of pathways through successive settings. Even if learning in individual settings were to be less differentiated than argued above, individual 'learning careers' through a range of social settings would necessarily be highly differentiated.

This analysis is not an argument against the concept of situated learning, but against simplistic accounts of situated learning which both fail to recognise all the different types of learning taking place in many situations and to take into account the influences on every situation of the different learning histories the participants bring with them. To understand any situation involving several people it is necessary to adopt two complementary perspectives. One should focus on the situation itself – its antecedents, wider context and ongoing interaction with its environment – and on the transactions of its participants throughout the period of enquiry. The other should focus on the contribution of the situation to the learning careers of individual participants, the learning acquired during their 'visit'. From a situational perspective knowledge is already present in established activities and cultural norms and imported through the contributions of new participants. From an individual perspective, some of their prior knowledge is resituated in the new setting and integrated with other knowledge acquired through participation. According to the magnitude of the impact of the 'visit', their knowledge can be described as having been expanded, modified or even transformed.

This theoretical prospective can be applied to just two of the learning processes discussed earlier in this paper to gain a deeper understanding. First, learning from experience has traditionally been presented as a purely individual activity with other people being part of the experience rather than part of the learning: co-learners. The focus has been on the extraction from episodic memory of explicit descriptions of features of the experience and/or generalisable understandings of it and/or theories of action in that particular environment. The learning process is commonly described as a reflective process incorporating prior explicit knowledge as well as recent experience (and prior implicit knowledge). However, if the social nature of the

situation is acknowledged, this learning process becomes more complicated. Possible understandings may be embedded in the social dimension of the situation and possible actions may be available as types of activity already familiar to other participants. Others will bring their own prior knowledge, explicit or implicit, to discussions of events and their own personal interpretations. We learn that others know things that we do not know, and that we can rely on others to contribute to certain aspects of a situation and save our own mental effort. So the individual process of making personal sense of the situation is likely to draw on a much wider range of cognitive resources, whether this is recognised or not.

Another learning process involves the application of scientific knowledge, which is publicly available if not widely understood, to practical situations. Typically, the use of a concept or idea in a new situation will involve:

- understanding the situation, which itself may require appropriate use of some prior knowledge;

- recognising that the concept or idea is relevant;

- changing it into a form appropriate for the situation;

- integrating that knowledge with other knowledge in the planning and implementation of action.

The net result of this process is twofold: the knower's capacity to think and act is enhanced by the learning involved in making the concept or idea available for use in that type of situation; their personal knowledge of the concept is enriched and its meaning extended by it being resituated in a new situation. The meaning of a concept for its knower is embedded in a cluster of experiences of using it. This cluster is formed by successive episodes of knowledge use in different situations. It is reasonable to suggest that the most readily available examples will be those most frequently and/or most recently used, or those which made a critical impact at the time. While there will be some common features across a wide range of contexts of use and between knowers, there may also be considerable differences. Hence, what may begin as publicly available scientific knowledge, which people treat as having a universal meaning, may end up us a set of differentiated variations formed by the distinctly separate learning histories of a group of individuals. Adopting a socially situated perspective on knowledge may paradoxically lead to an even greater differentiation in the knowledge held by different knowers. It is also possible that the process of resituation will lead to something more than an expanded range of knowledge use: its integration with other knowledge may amount to an example of knowledge creation.

This variation in personal understanding of what scientists would usually regard as the same concept is not readily understood by the knowers. When questioned about the meaning of the concept they will usually offer an easily recognisable textbook definition. Their knowledge of how to use the concept in practical situations will typically be tacit. They will be aware that it took some time before they found themselves able to use the concept, but will have little recollection of how this came about. This theory helps us to recognise that transfer is the learning process involved in resituating some aspect of one's knowledge into a new context, and that such a process subtly changes the meaning cluster of the knowledge being transferred. But will such recognition make this learning any more explicit?

Conclusions

This chapter has identified several different types of situation in which tacit knowledge may be either acquired or used or simultaneously both acquired and used. These are:

- knowledge acquired by implicit learning of which the knower is unaware;
- knowledge constructed from the aggregation of episodes in long-term memory;
- knowledge inferred by observers to be capable of representation as implicit theories of action, personal constructs, schemas, etc;
- knowledge that enables rapid, intuitive understanding or response;
- knowledge entailed in transferring knowledge from one situation to another;
- knowledge embedded in taken-for-granted activities, perceptions and norms.

Sometimes more than one of these characteristics will be present in the same situation. It could be argued that the last type is a subset of the first, but none of the other categories is subsumed by another in spite of many areas of overlap. Most of them are more likely to occur in non-formal settings, although such knowledge acquisition also occurs unobserved in the interstices of formal learning contexts. Tidy images of knowledge and learning are usually deceptive.

Having spent some time considering whether and when tacit knowledge might be made explicit and exploring some of the imminent difficulties, the question of why we should want to make tacit knowledge more explicit if it still enables us to do things also needs to be addressed. Apart from the scholar's natural drive to convert all available knowledge into publications, four good practical reasons come to mind:

- to improve the quality of a person's or a team's performance;
- to help to communicate knowledge to another person;
- to keep your actions under critical control by linking aspects of performance with more and less desirable outcomes;
- to construct artefacts that can assist decision making or reasoning.

Improvement of performance is particularly dependent on feedback. This can both contribute to confidence and fluency and draw attention to aspects that might be improved. The latter depends on the performer receiving some message, or making a self-diagnosis, that suggests some alterations to his or her performance which are feasible and have a net positive effect. This requires statements about the performance which indicate with sufficient clarity just what aspect might be improved, but does not necessarily require a description of that performance. The frequent use of video-recordings by coaches suggests that brief comments on the content of a video are more effective than extended verbal criticism. The coach can stop and point and repeat a video episode to ensure that all observers including the performer(s) are looking at and talking about the same thing, and not distracted by unimportant surface features of what is shown. It is reasonable to argue that a video and critique of a performance convey both explicit and tacit knowledge, even when the explicit aspect is only partly verbal. The expertise of the coach lies as much in the selection of material for closer observation and comment as in the comment itself, an aspect of knowledge that is easily taken for granted but becomes more obvious when one considers the role of a film director. In the absence of any recording, the description of a situation or event is a highly skilled activity; we admire the ability of a short story writer to disclose meaning in apparently ordinary activities, but we may not find it in our colleagues.

So far the focus has been on the problem of characterising the know-how embedded in action. The tacit knowledge that may lie behind the action raises the rather different problem of trying to explain perceptions. Recording can only show excerpts of time and space as seen from a particular position and direction: the whole picture is not available, and how do you know just where and when to look? The performer's own account of what they did and why can be challenged for several reasons. The account may be sparse, large tracts of taken-for-granted information will normally be excluded, their attention when performing will not be focused on remembering current action but deciding what to do next, accounts will be tidied up and subject to post-hoc rationalisation and so on (Nisbett and Wilson, 1977; Tomlinson, 1999). The observer has no access to the performer's thoughts or knowledge base.

A degree of explicitness is needed not only for improving performance but also for accountability purposes. Some linkage between actions and outcomes is necessary if a person is to take responsibility for his or her actions. However, the limitations to making tacit knowledge explicit are formidable, and much of the discussion about it in the literature is ill-informed if not naive. Geertz (1973), an American anthropologist, used the term 'thick' description to characterise the outcome of ethnographic research in contrast to more conventional, less time-consuming approaches. Using this to interpret the phenomenon of practical knowledge it can be said that *thick* tacit versions of personal knowledge coexist with *thin* explicit versions: the thick version is used in practice, the thin version for describing and justifying that practice.

Early on in this chapter we discussed the problem of researchers finding out about the knowledge of experts, situations where circumstances increased the probability of knowledge being shared among performers and techniques whereby researchers could begin to learn a little more about the knowledge that underpins performance. There could be many benefits for making some progress in this area and it is worthwhile pursuing the problem of eliciting tacit or near-tacit knowledge. However, it would be unwise to expect the sudden revelations which some authors have glibly predicted. For educators and policy makers the implications are rather different. They have to accept and understand the large role played by tacit knowledge in all parts of our lives and avoid the delusion of hyper-rational interpretations of professional action. If people's tacit personal knowledge and implicit learning are devalued, their confidence will diminish and their use of, and interest in, more formal knowledge will also suffer.

References

Argyris, C. and Schön, D.A. (1974) *Organizational learning: A theory in action perspective*, Reading, MA: Addison-Wesley.

Benner, P. (1984) *From novice to expert: Excellence and power in clinical nursing practice*, Menlo Park, CA: Addison-Wesley.

Berry, D.C. (ed) (1997) *How implicit is implicit learning?*, Oxford: Oxford University Press.

Dewey, J. (1933) *How we think – A restatement of the relation of reflective thinking to the educative process*, Boston, MA: Heath.

Dreyfus, H.L. and Dreyfus, S.E. (1986) *Mind over machine: The power of human intuition and expertise in the era of the computer*, Oxford: Basil Blackwell.

Eraut, M. (1994) *Developing professional knowledge and competence*, London: Falmer Press.

Eraut, M. (1995) 'Schön shock: a case for reframing reflection-in-action?', *Teachers and Teaching*, vol 1, no 1, pp 9-22.

Eraut, M. (1997) 'Perspectives on defining "the learning society"', *Journal of Education Policy*, vol 12, no 6, pp 551-8.

Eraut, M. (1999) 'Professional knowledge, practice and mode of cognition', in R.A. Foucher (ed) *Proceedings of international conference on self-directed learning*, Montreal.

Eraut, M., Alderton, J., Boylan, A. and Wraight, A. (1995) *Learning to use scientific knowledge in education and practice settings*, London: English National Board for Nursing, Midwifery and Health Visiting.

Eraut, M., Alderton, J., Cole, G. and Senker, P. (1998) *Development of knowledge and skills in employment*, Research Report No 5, Brighton: Institute of Education, University of Sussex.

Fox, R.D., Mazmanian, P. and Putnam, R.W. (1989) *Changing and learning in the lives of physicians*, New York, NY: Praeger.

Gear, J., McIntosh, A. and Squires, G. (1994) *Informal learning in the professions*, Hull: School of Education, University of Hull.

Geertz, C. (1973) 'Thick description: toward an interpretive theory of culture', in C. Geertz, *The interpretation of culture: Selective essays*, New York, NY: Basic Books, pp 3-32.

Hammersley, M. (1997) 'Educational research and teaching: a response to David Hargreaves' TTA lecture', *British Educational Research Journal*, vol 23, no 2, pp 141-61.

Holland, J.H., Holyoak, K.J., Nisbett, R.E. and Thagard, P.R. (1986) *Induction: Processes of inference, learning and discovery*, Cambridge, MA: MIT Press.

Horvath, J.A., Sternberg, R.J., Forsythe, G.B., Bullis, R.C., Williams, W.M. and Sweeney, P.J. (1996) 'Implicit theories of leadership practice', Paper presented at Annual Meeting of AERA, New York, 10 April.

Jackson, P.W. (1971) 'The way teachers think', in G.S. Lesser (ed) *Psychology and educational practice*, Chicago, IL: Scott Foresman, pp 10-34.

Kaplan, A. (1964) *The conduct of inquiry, methodology for behavioral science*, San Francisco, CA: Chandler.

Kelly, G.A. (1955) *The psychology of personal constraints*, vols 1 and 2, New York, NY: W.M. Norton.

Klein, G.A. (1989) 'Recognition-primed decisions', in W.B. Rouse (ed) *Advances in man-machine systems research*, Greenwich, CT: Jai Press, pp 47-92.

Klein, G.A., Oranasu, J., Calderwood, R. and Zsambok, C.E. (1993) *Decision-making in action: Models and methods*, Norwood, NJ: Ablex.

Knowles, M.S. (1970) *The modern practice of adult education: Andragogy versus pedagogy*, Chicago, IL: Follett.

Kolb, D. (1984) *Experiential learning*, Englewood Cliffs, NJ: Prentice Hall.

Long, H.B. and associates (1996) *Current developments in self-directed learning*, Oklahoma: College of Education, University of Oklahoma.

McCall, M.W., Lombardo, M.M. and Morrison, A.M. (1988) *The lessons of experience: How successful executives develop on the job*, Lexington, MA: Lexington Books.

McMaster University, Evidence-Based Medicine Working Group (EBMWG) (1992) 'Evidence-based medicine: a new approach to teaching the practice of medicine', *Journal of the American Medical Association*, vol 268, no 17, pp 2420-5.

Marsick, V.J. and Watkins, K.E. (1990) *Informal and incidental learning in the workplace*, London: Routledge.

Megginson, D. (1996) 'Planned and emergent learning: consequences for development', *Management Learning*, vol 27, no 4, pp 411-28.

Molander, B. (1992) 'Tacit knowledge and silenced knowledge: fundamental problems and controversies', in B. Göranzon and M. Florin (eds) *Skill and education: Reflection and experience*, Springer-Verlag, pp 9–31.

Mumford, A., Robinson, G. and Stradling, D. (undated) *Developing directors: The learning process*, Buckingham: International Management Centre, University of Buckingham.

Nisbett, R.E. and Wilson, T.D. (1977) 'Telling more than we can know: verbal reports on mental processes', *Psychology Review*, vol 84, no 3, pp 231–59.

Polanyi, M. (1967) *The tacit dimension*, Garden City, NY: Doubleday.

Reber, A.S. (1993) *Implicit learning and tacit knowledge: An essay on the cognitive unconscious*, Oxford: Oxford University Press.

Salomon, G. (ed) (1993) *Distributed cognition: Psychological and educational considerations*, Cambridge: Cambridge University Press.

Schön, D. (1983) *The reflective practitioner: How professionals think in action*, New York, NY: Basic Books.

Spender, J.-C. (1995) 'Organizational knowledge, learning and memory: three concepts in search of a theory', *Journal of Organizational Change Management*.

Spender, J.-C. (1998) 'The dynamics of individual and organizational knowledge', in C. Eden, J.-C. Spender (eds) *Managerial and organisational cognition*, London: Sage Publications, pp 13–39.

Straka, G.A. (ed) (1997) *European views of self-directed learning*, Münster, FRG: Waxmann.

Tomlinson, P. (1999) 'Conscious reflection and implicit learning: towards a balance in teacher preparation', *Oxford Review of Education*, December.

Tough, A.M. (1971) *The adult's learning projects*, Toronto: Ontario Institute for Studies in Education.

Tulving, E. (1972) 'Episodic and semantic memory', in E. Tulving and W. Donaldson (eds) *Organization of memory*, New York, NY: Academic Press, pp 382–403.

Underwood, G. (ed) (1996) *Implicit cognition*, Oxford: Oxford University Press.

Webber, P. (1999) 'The impact on academic and workplace learning of problem-focused Masters Degree Courses in Management', Paper presented at annual conference, British Educational Research Association, Brighton, 5 September, pp 11–16.

Weinstein, M.C. and Fineberg, H.V. (1980) *Clinical decision analysis*, Philadelphia, PA: W.B. Saunders.

2

Informal learning and social capital

John Field and Lynda Spence

This chapter analyses the relationship between aspects of the social order and the propensity to engage in organised learning. Conventional wisdom and scholarly consensus alike suggest that the higher the level of education initially received, the greater the likelihood of learning across the lifespan. This does not appear to be the case in Northern Ireland and only partly the case in Scotland. Our research is concerned with establishing the extent of and reasons for this apparent divergence (Field and Schuller, 1995). One of our findings is that low levels of participation in formal education and training can simply mean that people have found that informal learning is a better way of achieving the goals they set themselves. This seems to be associated with the phenomenon that is sometimes known as 'social capital' – namely the existence of networks, norms and levels of trust that promote collective action between members of a given social grouping. This argument, while developed in order to explain the divergence that we have found in Northern Ireland, and to a less marked extent in Scotland, has evident applicability elsewhere.

Implicit in the concept of a 'learning society' is the idea that social arrangements can shape and influence people's attitudes towards learning. Concentrating largely on the evidence from Northern Ireland, this chapter suggests that the relationship may take unexpected forms. In the case of Northern Ireland, at least, a high level of networking and communal trust (albeit within two partly segregated ethnic/religious divisions) may help to explain a relatively low level of participation in formal adult learning opportunities.

Northern Ireland – a pattern of divergence?[1]

In what has long been a standard text on adult learning, Cross concluded that:

Of all the variables that have been related to educational interest and participation, amount of formal schooling has more influence than any other.... In short, learning is addictive; the more education people have, the more they want, and the more they will get. (Cross, 1981, pp 54-5)

This conclusion has attained almost canonical status among adult education specialists. It has been repeatedly confirmed by researchers since Cross, and in a variety of different socioeconomic settings. The Organisation for Economic Co-operation and Development (OECD), in its recent 12-country international study of adult literacy, confirmed yet again that:

Participation in adult education and training increases with the level of education initially received: the higher the level, the more likely a person is to participate. (OECD, 1997, p 94)

This conclusion has often been held to entail a number of policy consequences. For example, if adult learning follows on from initial educational level, it makes sense to tackle schooling deficiencies as the major element in any long-term strategy for combating illiteracy and building capacities for lifelong learning. It may also make sense to use indices of initial educational achievement to measure the potential stock of human capital at any one time.

Evidence of a divergence in Northern Ireland is not hard to come by. What is remarkable is the fact that it was ignored for such a long time, both by policy makers and by researchers. For many years, the Northern Ireland government preferred not to dwell on the evidence of low participation in continuing education and training. The Training and Enterprise Agency's (TEA) contribution to the UK Skills Audit stressed that:

Overall NI compares well against the UK as a whole in terms of new entrants to the labour force in terms of both NVQ levels 2 and 3. This is a more useful comparison than comparing the labour force as a whole since it reflects current trends in education and training provision. (DfEE/Cabinet Office, 1996, p 64)

Behind this remarkable complacency lay the government's desire to attract inward investment into Northern Ireland. In a typical promotional statement in 1997, the Industrial Development Board listed '10 Good Reasons to Invest in Northern Ireland', the second of them being "A reliable, adaptable and well-educated labour force" (IDB, 1997). While the incoming Labour government started to acknowledge that lifelong learning presented a considerable challenge in Northern Ireland, the 1998 consultation over its policy proposals was low-key and presented largely as an offshoot of the British Green Papers (TEA/DENI, 1998; DENI, 1998; Worthington, 1998). Nevertheless, this was the first time on record that senior policy makers had acknowledged Northern Ireland's poor record on adult learning.

In view of the scholarly consensus over initial education and later participation, this pattern should come as something of a surprise. Initial educational attainment in Northern Ireland is comparatively high, at least by British standards. This can be measured relatively simply, since most pupils in Northern Ireland schools take the same academic and vocational qualifications as their British counterparts. Table 1 summarises the picture in 1995/96, but the same broad pattern has been apparent throughout the last decade: both in GCSEs and A levels, the performance of Northern Ireland pupils at the upper end has clearly outstripped that

of British pupils. At the other end of the attainment league table, in recent years the proportion of Northern Ireland school leavers who have no graded examinations results has fallen well below the UK average (Table 2). Northern Ireland school leavers are more likely to enter higher education than their counterparts in England and Wales; Northern Ireland is the only UK region where significant numbers of children from manual working-class backgrounds go on to enter higher education (Field, 1997b). While these overall statistics conceal marked regional variations as well as some areas of weakness (Field, 1999), it is still reasonable to conclude that exam performance in Northern Ireland is consistently higher than in the rest of the UK.

Table 1: Qualifications gained by pupils in Northern Ireland and England (1995-96) (%)

	NI	England
5 or more GCSEs at levels A-C	51.6	44.5
2 or more A Levels	35.9	29.6

Source: Pullinger (1998)

Table 2: School leavers with no graded GCSE results in Northern Ireland and the UK (1994/95) (%)

NI	4.4
UK	7.9

Source: Pullinger (1997)

Recorded participation in adult learning, by contrast, is comparatively weak. As noted above, this runs counter to received wisdom, so the evidence warrants some attention. The most recent survey data for general adult participation comes from the 1996 adult learning survey; this showed that 52% of adults reported having done no organised learning since leaving school, compared with 36% in the UK as a whole; 62% said they were unlikely to take up learning in the foreseeable future, compared with 54% in Britain; non-participants in Northern Ireland were more likely to cite 'lack of interest' as a factor than were British respondents (Field, 1997a, pp 92-5).

Data from the Labour Force Survey (LFS) are consistent with this overall picture. Those who are in employment are less likely to receive training than are British employees: in spring 1996, for example, less than 5% of manual workers in Northern Ireland underwent training in the four-week period under study, compared with 9% for the UK as a whole; the figures for non-manual workers were 12% and 18% respectively (Pullinger, 1997). The LFS also shows that the Northern Ireland workforce is considerably less likely to possess formal qualifications than is the case in Britain (Table 3). In fact, all the available evidence points in the same direction: fewer adults take part in organised learning in Northern Ireland than elsewhere in the UK.

Table 3: Share of the UK workforce without any formal qualifications (spring 1997) (%)

Region/nation	
Northern Ireland	26.9
Wales	23.5
England	18.2
Scotland	17.5

Source: Pullinger (1997)

A review of the quantitative evidence confirms, then, the existence of a clear divergence between (high) levels of initial attainment and (low) levels of adult participation. We will be presenting the evidence on Scotland in other publications; in summary, there appears to be less divergence in Scotland, but on the other hand neither does it display a straightforwardly positive association between initial attainment and adult participation. This suggests that there may be merit in extending this aspect of the analysis to other regions, in England and Wales, as well as to different areas within Scotland.

In explaining the Northern Ireland divergence, some weight must be given to what might be called structural factors. These would include emigration patterns, particularly among the 40% of higher education entrants who study in Britain and rarely return upon graduation (Gallagher et al, 1996). Patterns of employment are also important: the Northern Ireland labour market is strongly marked by the relative strength of the public sector; and of

the small firms sector, including a very large number of family units such as farms. The latter in particular are less likely to invest in training than are larger privately-owned enterprises. However, structural factors such as these cannot explain everything. Even comparing like with like, the trend in Northern Ireland is a distinctive one: thus the Gallup survey found that even members of social categories ABC1 are less likely to participate in learning than is the case in Britain (Field, 1997a, p 92). We therefore turn to a discussion of social relationships and values, in an attempt to explore their possible influence on this pattern.

Social networks, norms and trust

Social capital is still a relatively recent concept. By contrast the notion of human capital is a well-known one, both as a theoretical concept and as a policy concept that influences public priorities. At the heart of human capital theory is the idea that when individuals, organisations and nations allocate resources to education and training, they can expect measurable returns on this investment. The concept of social capital is less well-known, and its definition is still under debate (Edwards and Foley, 1997).

Originally associated with the work of Bourdieu, its early usage was in connection with the old-boy type networks that are enjoyed by professional and elite groups to promote their careers and advance their political interests (Bourdieu, 1977, p 503). More recently, Coleman (1994) and Putnam (1993) have extended the concept, which in their work encompasses the networks, norms and shared sense of trust that are available as resources to any group of actors, and not solely elites. It is in this sense that our project has adapted the concept to the study of lifelong learning (see Table 4).

Putnam and Coleman both define and operationalise the notion of social capital in slightly different ways. For Coleman, social capital is the "set of resources that inhere in family relations and in community social organisation and that are useful for the cognitive or social development of a child or young person" (1994, p 300). In a set of empirical studies of denominational schools in the United States, Coleman tried to demonstrate that the strong bonds between school, family, church and neighbourhood may provide more powerful

Table 4: Varieties of social capital

	Source	Institutional form	Benefit or function	Ownership
Bourdieu	Form of accumulated labour	Personal contacts	Social reproduction and capital accumulation	Individual
Coleman	Social relationships	Family, church, voluntary organisations	Educational achievements	Community
Putnam	Collectively-allocated resources	Voluntary associations, political forums	Prosperity and civic reciprocity	Community

influences on young people's attainments than parental social class or school type. Putnam's emphasis is slightly different, conceptually and empirically. Although Putnam is certainly interested in education, his preoccupation in this respect is more with the capacity of any given society to share its collective learning in ways that bear fruit in terms of collective activity; for Putnam, the types of resources that are available as a result of social capital are decisive in determining levels of stability and prosperity. Social capital functions beneficially because it fosters high expectations of reciprocity, facilitates information flows, penalises those who do not communicate and cooperate, and embodies the fruits of past successful collaboration (Putnam, 1993, p 173).

How might this social capital interact with lifelong learning? Superficially, its influence may appear to be unambiguously positive, particularly if you pursue the Bourdieu model of social capital as a narrow asset available to elites. It might be assumed that the more social capital the greater the payoffs from lifelong learning. This might be a plausible and logical sequence, but for the fact that social capital can offer both a complement and an alternative to education and training as a means of attaining both individual and group goals. The collective sanctions available to actors may be used against those who take part in some types of education and training; high levels of trust and strong networks can be associated with a tendency to promote informal learning through members of the family or neighbourhood or workforce. In his studies of networks in operation, Granovetter emphasises the importance of what he calls 'weak ties'. In contrast with 'strong ties', which can provide a powerful deterrent to innovation and creativity, 'weak ties' are often ephemeral and

operate across a relatively narrow front (1973). Thus family-based networks may foster business conservatism and hinder innovation; but business acquaintances who are known in one context can provide favours in another without risking disruption and destabilisation of the relationship. Taking Granovetter's thinking a step further, it could be hypothesised that in certain circumstances, high levels of social capital will foster high levels of informal learning and low levels of participation in formal education and training. One key ingredient in the equation will then be the extent to which education and training systems themselves are an embedded aspect of the networks and trust which provide such effective resources in attaining group goals. Instead of a simple linear model, a more complex set of alternative relationships are available (see Figure 1).

Figure 1: Two models of social capital and lifelong learning

Education and training system weakly integrated into wider networks

Social capital	Adult learning
Weak ties prevalent	Formal – high participation Informal – low participation
Strong ties prevalent	Formal – low participation Informal – high participation

Formal education and training system strongly integrated into wider networks

Social capital	Adult learning
Weak ties prevalent	Formal – high participation Informal – high participation
Strong ties prevalent	Formal – high participation Informal – low participation

Situating an entire society on this spectrum – even such a small and compact one as Northern Ireland – is no easy matter. However, it can be suggested that taken as a whole, the population of Northern Ireland appears to enjoy relatively high levels of social capital, based on strong ties. The evidence for this includes survey findings that demonstrate – in comparison with Britain and several other Western European societies – a marked tendency towards collectivism; high levels of church attendance; low levels of family breakdown, with a divorce rate well below the English and Scottish levels; and strong support for charities and voluntary organisations. At the same time, access to social capital is sharply divided along ethnic–religious lines: networks and trust do not cross the community division, and are in part a protective measure against the variety of threats which are perceived to arise from uncertainty (Field, 1999). On a number of key (albeit proxy) measures there are reasonable grounds for concluding that there are comparatively high levels of social capital in Northern Ireland, that this in turn rests on 'close' and dense ties, and that its contours follow the wider rift within Northern Ireland society.

These differential aspects of social capital are important in exploring the distinctive patterns of adult education and training in Northern Ireland. At the level of initial education, the idea that high attainment has something to do with the intensive and multiple socialisation of young people by family, church and community leaders, seems highly plausible. In the course of our fieldwork, the family in particular was said by professionals to be a key factor in the academic attainment of young people, and it was generally accepted that church and local community leaders were likely to underpin this function. It may also be concluded that social capital offers accessible and familiar routes for occupational advance and consumer enjoyment: compared with the risks and uncertainties of entering a formal institution for a period of retraining or upskilling, family, neighbours and local associations offer a far less painful way of achieving desired objectives. In this sense, the 'dense ties' of Northern Ireland mean that schooling is for the young, and it is geared largely towards entry to higher education. By contrast, by providing an alternative set of resources for achieving individual

and group goals for adults, social capital can inhibit participation in adult learning.

Placing informal learning in Northern Ireland

Empirical evidence for these assertions comes from a variety of sources. In particular, it is drawn from 10 sectoral focus groups and 25 semi-structured interviews, which form part of our research study carried out in 1997 and 1998. Both focus groups and individual interviews involved people with formal responsibilities for human resources issues; for some, training or education constituted their continued professional role, and for others it was one among many responsibilities. The aim of both focus groups and interviews was to consider a number of aspects of the relationship between initial and continuing education, and to explore the reasons for participation patterns among adults[2].

Themes from the empirical data highlighted in this section include: a possible preference for informal methods of selection and recruitment in the labour market in Northern Ireland; the influence of the family on attitudes to education and training; the combination of a strong preference for informal learning with uncertainty about its currency. Our findings with respect to the more negative aspects of social capital will also be considered briefly.

As an example, let us consider the role of social capital in the labour market. Here, it might be expected that strong social capital will favour the use of informal methods of selection and deployment (personal contacts, recommendations and direct knowledge) rather than formal ones (advertisements, specified qualifications). This runs directly up against Northern Ireland's employment legislation, which is somewhat more detailed and prescriptive than is common elsewhere in Europe. The fair employment laws provide for the use of strict and transparent criteria in selection for employment decisions, in order to encourage equality of employment opportunity between the communities. One interviewee, a voluntary sector manager, stated:

"Certainly if we employ anyone, and we publicly advertise, which we do, we are very careful to make sure that the qualifications are exactly spelled out ... also we would be very meticulous about that we need five years' work experience or whatever we need, and that is being spelled out.... We want people who have the proper qualifications and experience." (Interviewee)

On the other hand, there are two important notes of caution. Firstly, fair employment legislation is more strictly observed in some areas than others; it is largely accepted as legitimate in the voluntary/ community sector and among the larger externally-owned companies and in parts of the public sector; in some other parts of the economy, it may be seen by managers as a hindrance to flexibility and competitiveness. Secondly, only firms and organisations employing 11 or more people are required to register with the Fair Employment Commission. While any employer can be prosecuted for discriminatory employment practices, the more stringent procedures which govern recruitment in larger firms do not necessarily apply to the same extent in the small business sector, including farms, where many Northern Ireland people find employment. If so, there may be more scope for selecting employees by informal means, such as personal knowledge or recommendation.

Our focus group evidence suggested that even in the public sector reputation may still carry more weight than academic qualifications. As one health service manager explained:

"If you're living in a bigger area, say England or Scotland, the need for your career progression – I've no evidence but experience – but it may well depend to a higher level on your academic progression than here in Northern Ireland where your competency or the way people talk about you, you know, 'He or she did a good job then', that may play [other group member: uh huh] a much stronger role [third member: that's true]." (Public Sector Healthcare Focus Group)

What is true for labour, incidentally, is also true for other managerial decisions, particularly on a day-to-day basis: purchasing, marketing and financing strategies may be shaped by the existence of alternative ways of getting results. This business

sector interviewee laid great emphasis on the role of personal contact within the business community:

"If I'm doing business with an individual I haven't met before, they don't know anything about me, they very much like the sound of my product, they see the company as sound, but I am not part of their own network. They will pick up the telephone and network to find out if any other person has heard of me. Basically, they're taking a reference. And based on that person's word, they will do business with me.... You can get further by asking someone to make a phone call than you ever could through an excellent presentation, by standing up and doing a sales talk. It sounds good, but I'll only buy your product if I know someone else who does, and likes it. Personal recommendation is very strong (here). It's a very different way of doing business than in the UK [sic]." (Interviewee)

Our fieldwork suggests that family strongly favours achievement in school (somewhat traditionally defined), but may directly and indirectly inhibit participation in lifelong learning. Interviewees were often divided as to the importance of the family in relation to initial continuing education. While most stressed the importance of parents in encouraging children towards educational achievement, others feared that in certain marginalised geographical areas and communities, little importance was attached to education. One expert in equality issues feared that the undue influence of older family members perpetuated stereotypical job choices by girls (Interview). On the other hand, the chief executive of a training organisation in a deprived urban area had this to say about parental interest and influence when a new firm was about to open locally:

"Mothers have come to me and said, 'How can I get my child ready to be in a position to apply for that job?' I think that's marvellous, because that's at a very micro level. Then a group of parents get together and they want information about things. You're able to tell them, this is what X are looking for, and very often it's not just about vocational skills.... Parents can understand those concepts ... so even if they leave vocational training and the academic qualifications to educationalists and training providers, they can certainly get the young person's mind set in the right place.... It's the parents who persuade them to get in to work, when they prefer to lie in bed because they've got a little bit of a sniffle.

Parents are influential and they understand, if they have a job, it's important to hold on to a job. While they live at home ... the parent can be that essential link between the employer and the individual and learning objectives." (Interviewee)

When it came to adult learning, there was a sense that close family ties inhibited a constant reinvestment in the self. There was little disagreement with the view that, once in a job, it was sensible to stay where you were. One exchange between focus group participants on this topic suggests that this is not a simple matter of economic security:

A: *"... the pressure from the parents is always to get a good education and you'll be made for life ... when you've got a job, you know, you don't go mucking about with that, you daren't tell your mother you're thinking of moving. 'Sure, you've got a good job and you're there for life, you stay there'. I think that's part of the psyche that's in us...."*

B: *"That's the PPP, you've got a permanent pensionable post [yep], that my mother used to talk about [yes]."* (Software Industry Focus Group)

Participants in focus groups were somewhat reticent on the subject of schooling, or more accurately, about the subject of selection at 11. Take the following exchange:

"... particularly if you get a grammar education, and you get A levels, that's nearly as far as you need to go. I think there's still a bit of a throwback there, from that.... And if you get a job, like in the civil service through that, you don't really need to study any further [general hubbub]." (Rural Development Focus Group)

A throwaway remark about civil service employment was treated by other participants as controversial; by contrast, the reference to grammar schools was not picked up. On the few occasions when selection was raised by an individual participant others in the focus group would normally remain silent or change the subject. Interviewees were less reticent, many identifying failure in the 11-plus examination as having a negative effect on attitudes to lifelong learning. This prominent academic spoke of the long-term effects

on her confidence of not even being entered for the examination:

"I was at post-graduate level – and with a first class degree – and still lacking confidence in myself.... If you're told you're stupid at a young age or if that impression is given to you, for some of us that does put a marker down."

It was generally taken for granted that failing the transfer test was a humiliating experience that marked you for life ("they made you feel stupid": female participant, speaking about her secondary school teachers, Rural Development Focus Group).

Social capital was strongly associated throughout this study with a marked preference among adults for informal rather than formal learning. On a number of occasions, focus groups and interviewees voiced mild misgivings or stronger criticisms about the formal further education sector (particularly outside Belfast). This interviewee was concerned that the formal education system stifled initiative in relation to continued learning:

"If you have someone who has been conditioned to listen, to let someone feed them knowledge, it's a bit like a dependency culture on grants, or charity, that you sit back and wait for someone to say something to you, rather than having the initiative to say, I want to go and learn." (Interviewee)

Strong claims on behalf of the voluntary and community sector – particularly in relation to women learners – went largely unchallenged in the focus groups. The contrast was expressed starkly by one rural development specialist:

"I think the other factor is the joy in learning.... And I think that has been created to some extent through the women's groups, you know, where there is a bit of fun involved, and it's social, and so on, and you can relatively easily mix different tasks, job skills, individually and sharing experience, and so on. It's a much broader sort of milieu." (Rural Development Focus Group)

Others in the group spoke vividly of learning from experience, by watching others, and by asking people questions. This was contrasted with the allegedly forbidding visual image of the local further education institute (FEI), a point later reinforced in an interview with a department head in one such institute, who worried that:

> "... the conditions maybe don't help and students at the margins, who maybe have this lack of confidence, who have felt that they were always second best, come into the place and they're put into rooms where it looks second best, [and] it just reinforces [their previous experience]." (Interviewee)

Apparently, few FEIs have close contacts with employers (Grant Thornton, 1998), and outside Belfast, the FEIs recruit a largely youthful student population, providing few opportunities for adult returners (DENI, 1998).

On our evidence, successful recruitment to continuing education in Northern Ireland, whether formal or informal, is linked to informal information sharing and trust. The above interviewee also spoke of the importance of word-of-mouth recommendation among learners, rather than conventional methods of advertising, as a means of attracting people into further education. The significance of word-of-mouth recommendation mirrors the findings of another project in the ESRC *Learning Society Programme*, which showed that the majority of young people considering further education in one London suburb relied very heavily on local family-friendship networks for information and advice (Ball et al, 1999). One of our interviewees, a union official who had successfully run Return to Learn courses for "the shop floor workers [who] hadn't had the same opportunities in education and training as the senior managers", also discovered that participation built up through student recommendation. This interviewee referred to what he believed to be a:

> "... healthy scepticism in Northern Ireland people. You know, 'what's this about...? Is it about the employer using me even more?'." (Interviewee)

His response was to take time out to convince potential students, through personal discussion, that there would be a personal development dividend for them.

Finally, our findings suggest that while social capital represents an important set of resources for informal learning, it also has limits and drawbacks. This was apparent from the very process of undertaking the fieldwork: for many of the participants the focus groups covered fresh and unfamiliar terrain, and following the formal closure of the group, we frequently found that people went beyond the bounds of normal politeness in thanking us for inviting them, describing the event in positive terms as stimulating and informative. This suggests that although networking and trust may be high, social capital does have a marked downside. The very informality of proceeding through contacts and personal approaches may mean that: much is routinely taken for granted; information is not shared consistently and uniformly; accepted 'authorities' go unchallenged; trust is withheld. An example is a community educator's opinion that there are "some very isolated people who are happy to be isolated". To make links between people and groups,

> "You need imagination and I think that's what's lacking and also what's lacking in getting everybody working together is the fear of what it will mean for that particular group to get involved. They'll want to know, first of all, what they're going to get from it and then they'll want to know what the demands on them will be." (Interviewee)

In this sense, opportunities for collective learning can be skewed or even blocked; sectarian communal divisions may be reinforced by entrenching mutual ignorance and negative stereotyping; the learning which takes place informally passes unrecognised by the wider world, and may indeed suffer from 'black holes' derived from an overreliance upon a narrow range of contacts.

Conclusion: some implications

All too often, talk of a 'learning society' or 'learning culture' fails to address in any detail the socially embedded nature of learning. This is as important in understanding young people's learning as it is in the case of adults, and Coleman's emphasis on social capital as a factor in schools attainment marks an important recognition of this fact. This chapter has taken a rather wider approach to the study of social capital than Coleman, particularly in suggesting that it may have a downside as well as an upside, and that it influences adults' behaviour as much as young people's. Nor is this by any means unique to Northern Ireland. Recently there has been growing recognition of the role of social capital as a resource that may influence the range of options open to young adults (Emler and McNamara, 1996; Furlong et al, 1996; Viscarret, 1998). Social capital can embody a range of resources that provide a credible and attractive way of pursuing collective goals for adults throughout their lifespans, and that this may create a strong preference for informal learning rather than formal provision. One consequence is that, in the fields of research and policy alike, there is a need to rethink the traditional focus on the supply of formal provision and certification; while it may be difficult to identify robust indicators of informal learning, these potentially offer an important contribution to the accurate measurement of human capital. In many contexts, particularly in small societies such as Northern Ireland, informal learning will often be good enough.

Recognising that informal learning can be highly effective is not the same thing as romanticising it. Both social capital and informal learning have their drawbacks as well as their payoffs; the risk is that as societies move to embrace the idea and practice of continuous lifelong learning, a reliance on non-formal learning will not simply generate and perpetuate inequality; it may (if unintentionally) legitimate those inequalities that arise from an unequal access to (recognised) knowledge (Beck, 1997). Similarly, community development strategies which reinforce locally-based and familial networks may inadvertently diminish the local capacity for accessing resources through wider but looser ties. This study suggests that if regions such as Northern Ireland are to embrace the informational, learning society, there will need to be a considerable effort to exploit the benefits from building functioning loose ties between the range of disparate stakeholders involved in strategic economic and cultural development activities. Particularly in Northern Ireland, those stakeholders include not only those who are widely accepted in Western Europe as the 'social partners' (employers, trade unions, professional associations) and the different layers of government; they will also need to embrace the community and voluntary sectors, with all that this implies for potential conflicts arising from differential access to power. This analysis of social capital confirms the relative weakness of networks that might serve as bridges between the community and voluntary sectors, particularly in excluded neighbourhoods, and the resources available through more conventional centres of political and economic power.

Finally, what of the schools? Evidently, initial education in Northern Ireland has been highly successful in preparing most young people for academic progress; but high academic standards have not helped to prepare the majority of the population for a life of continuous organised learning. Confronting this will also mean addressing the principle and practice of selection. Put simply, selection commands considerable support among parents and other stakeholders in Northern Ireland and there is little prospect of its immediate abolition. Not the least reason for the consensus in favour of selection is that in a community with comparatively strong social capital, the grammar schools have helped considerably in widening access to higher education among young people from working-class backgrounds, particularly among those from the Catholic community (Field, 1997b). Selection has also helped to keep the middle class in the state system, and given them a strong stake in its success.

Yet selection also has other consequences, including the demoralisation of those who are labelled (not least by themselves) as the learning failures. The trick in Northern Ireland will be to combine the strengths of selection while building pathways to lifelong learning for those who do not enter an academic track. This means a substantial increase in the value placed on vocational and work-based learning; it also means a greater awareness in schools of how best to benefit from and maximise the potential of the informal learning that exists among pupils, parents and teachers.

This study has attempted to sketch out something of the complexity of the relationship between social capital and lifelong learning. There appear to be good grounds for believing that strong social capital, based on dense ties of kin and community, is associated with high achievement in initial schooling and low participation in formal adult learning. What the present research also suggests is that strong social capital can help to sustain a lively culture of informal learning, but that the high value placed on formal academic achievement is not matched by an equal appreciation of the potential and efficacy of informal learning. This creates a complex and difficult set of challenges for policy makers; what is clear is that collectivist nostalgia – whether of the 'strong community' or the 'strong family' variety – is largely inappropriate. What is needed is a political strategy that tackles exclusion and economic decline by building wider, more inclusive, more open and looser ties – including but not limited to formal partnerships – between the range of stakeholders.

Notes

[1] This research was undertaken as part of a comparative study of 'Divergence between Initial and Continuing Education in Scotland and Northern Ireland'. Statistically, it appeared that there was in both countries a divergence between high levels of initial education and training on the one hand (as measured through attainment of qualifications at 16 and 18), and low levels of participation in adult learning on the other (as measured by participation in general adult education and vocational training). This pattern was reported in Field and Schuller (1995).

[2] In Northern Ireland, focus groups were conducted in the following sectors: private sector healthcare; public sector healthcare; financial industries; community and voluntary sector; agriculture; rural development; tourism and leisure; private sector training; electronics; and software. The interviews were held with 'stakeholders' in the education and training system, including those whose role was concerned with human resources issues at enterprise level and those with a primarily policy-oriented role. The interviewees came from outwith those sectors already studied through the focus groups.

References

Ball, S.J., Maguire, M. and Macrae, S. (1999) 'Whose Learning Society? The post-16 education and training market in one urban locale', Paper given to ESRC Conference on the Learning Society Programme, Church House, London, 6 July.

Beck, U. (1997) *Was ist Globalisierung?*, Frankfurt-am-Main: Suhrkamp Verlag.

Bourdieu, P. (1977) 'Cultural reproduction and social reproduction', in J. Karabel and A.H. Halsey (eds) *Power and ideology in education*, New York, NY: Oxford University Press, pp 487-511.

Coleman, J.S. (1994) *Foundations of social theory*, Cambridge: Belknap Press.

Cross, K.P. (1981) *Adults as learners: Increasing participation and facilitating learning*, San Francisco, CA: Jossey Bass.

DENI (Department of Education Northern Ireland) (1998) *Enrolments on vocational courses at Northern Ireland further education colleges*, Bangor: DENI.

DfEE (Department for Education and Employment)/Cabinet Office (1996) *The Skills Audit: A report from an interdepartmental group*, London: DfEE/Cabinet Office.

Edwards, B. and Foley, M. (1997) 'Social capital and the political economy of our discontent', *American Behavioural Scientist*, vol 40, no 5, pp 669-78.

Emler, N. and McNamara, S. (1996) 'The social contact patterns of young people', in H. Helve and J. Bynner (eds) *Youth and life management: Research perspectives*, Helsinki: Yliopistpaino, pp 121-39.

Field, J. and Schuller, T. (1995) 'Is there less adult learning in Scotland and Northern Ireland? A preliminary analysis', *Scottish Journal of Adult and Continuing Education*, vol 2, no 2, pp 71-80.

Field, J. (1997a) 'Northern Ireland - perspectives', in N. Sargant, J. Field, H. Francis, T. Schuller and A. Tuckett, *The learning divide*, Leicester: NIACE, pp 91-8.

Field, J. (1997b) 'Equity and access: adult participation in higher education in Northern Ireland', *Journal of Access Studies*, vol 12, no 2, pp 139-52.

Field, J. (1999) 'Human capital and social capital in Northern Ireland: linking schools achievement and lifelong learning', *Irish Educational Studies*, vol 18, pp 234-47.

Furlong, A., Biggart, A. and Cartmel, F. (1996) 'Neighbourhoods, opportunity structures and occupational aspirations', *Sociology*, vol 30, no 3, pp 551-65.

Gallagher, A.M., Osborne, R.D. and Cormack, R.J. (1996) *Attitudes to higher education: Report to Central Community Relations Unit and Department of Education*, Belfast: Centre for Research on Higher Education.

Granovetter, M. (1973) 'The strength of weak ties', *American Journal of Sociology*, vol 78, no 4, pp 1350-80.

Grant Thornton (1998) *Barometer of owner managed businesses in Northern Ireland*, Belfast: Grant Thornton.

IDB (1997) *Ten good reasons to invest in Northern Ireland*, Belfast: IDB.

OECD (Organisation for Economic Co-operation and Development) (1997) *Literacy skills for the knowledge society*, Paris: OECD.

Pullinger, J. (1997) *Regional Trends 32*, London: The Stationery Office.

Pullinger, J. (1998) *Regional Trends 33*, London: The Stationery Office.

Putnam, R.D. (1993) *Making democracy work: Civic traditions in modern Italy*, Princeton, NJ: Princeton University Press.

TEA (Training and Employment Agency) Department of Education Northern Ireland (DENI) (1998) *Lifelong learning*, Belfast/Bangor: TEA/DENI.

Viscarret, J.J. (1998) 'EU Programmes: a 'bridge' between education and employment', in A. Walther and B. Stauber (eds) *Lifelong learning in Europe: Options for the integration of living, learning and working*, Tübingen: Neuling Verlag, pp 242-7.

Worthington, T. (1998) 'New age for adult learning', *Belfast Telegraph*, 31 March, p 9.

3

Implicit knowledge, phenomenology and learning difficulties

Stephen Baron, Alastair Wilson and Sheila Riddell

Introduction

In a chapter in an earlier volume in this series we argued that the study of the marginalisation of adults with learning difficulties represented a strategic opportunity to explore the nature of a 'learning society' (Baron et al, 1998a). In particular, we suggested that studying skills from the perspective of the social model of disability would have a powerful dereifying effect. The social model of disability has, in the past decade, reconceptualised disability in terms of its being the product of barriers erected by current social relations to the full social participation of impaired people, rather than it being limitations caused by individual physical or mental impairments. This approach has been developed very largely with respect to people with physical impairments, wheelchair access being the classic issue. In the research reported here we are concerned with the application of this model to people with learning difficulties. Applying this perspective to people with learning disabilities in a learning society makes problematic central issues of learning, skills and knowledge. Rather than conceptualising these as objective phenomena, to be measured, judged and increased as necessary, the social model of disability sees these as social relations, specific to time, space and culture. From this perspective the question is not 'Does X have skill Y?' but 'How is X deemed to have attributes which are held to constitute skill Y and what consequences flow from this?' The implications for conceptualising a 'learning society' of such a change in perspective are profound.

In the earlier chapter we also argued that the study of supported employment projects would not only help us to understand the nature of skills more fully, but it would also help us to think the relationship between the utilitarian and the humanist tendencies in the working definition of a 'learning society' given in Baron et al (1998a). In this chapter we develop these arguments as the theoretical framework which we will use to explore the empirical case studies of adults with learning difficulties in supported employment, which we are currently conducting (Riddell et al, 1999).

We will first review the seminal work on the nature of skills and informal learning of Eraut et al (1998; see also Eraut's chapter in this volume) carried out as part of *The Learning Society Programme*. We will then draw from theoretical work in the phenomenological tradition on the acquisition of common sense (Schutz, 1976). From there we will analyse the history of supported employment, particularly in the United States and will then conclude with a consideration of the implications for definitions of The Learning Society.

Skills and informal learning

The work of Michael Eraut prior to, and in, *The Learning Society Programme* represents a sustained and systematic attempt to address the nature of knowledge in employment (Eraut, 1994; nd; Eraut et al, 1995, 1998; Chapter 1 of this volume). The focus on learning at work, rather than on courses and qualifications, leads the research away from the formalities of systems towards the informal and the processual (Eraut et al, 1998a, p 3; and Figure 1, Chapter 1 on p 14 of this volume). The conception of knowledge implied by this research agenda moves away from that of formal, propositional knowledge towards ideas of implicit, tacit or embedded knowledge, knowledge-in-action. This combines such public propositional knowledge with personally generated propositional knowledge and with skills. Eraut and his colleagues (hereafter referred to simply as Eraut) see such knowledge as inseparable from the process of its creation and application (Eraut et al,1998, p 5). In one direction this is a process in which explicit frameworks become implicit and semi-automatic as learning proceeds (Eraut, nd, pp 4-5) while, in the opposite direction, explicit knowledge might be derived from implicit knowledge (see p 21 of this volume). 'Capability', the preferred term for "the sum total of what [the person] can do" (Eraut, nd, p 4) is seen as something which is acquired (and can, in principle, be expanded) rather than something that is innate.

Such a reconceptualisation of the field of learning at work brings into play a range of first order questions about the social relations of knowledge and of work. The research claims, with justification, to be pioneering, "preparing the way for others to follow" (Eraut et al, 1998a, p 3). In engaging with this work we want to offer three major criticisms as the basis for the formulation of our study of supported employment for adults with learning difficulties.

First, the sampling which Eraut employed in *The Learning Society Programme* skewed the research in particular ways (Eraut et al, 1998a). The focus on three sectors, one manufacturing, one financial services/utility and one public, is defensible and holds the promise of allowing comparisons across different sites in the same sector. The sampling frames, the organisations from whom informants were drawn, ranged from 'medium-sized subsidiaries of US companies' (engineering), through NHS trusts based on district hospitals (public sector) to very large financial/utility organisations. The smallest sampled organisation would appear to be the medium-sized subsidiary of an international company, leaving smaller organisations, and the substantial proportion of the labour force which works in them, unsampled. Beyer and Kilsby estimate that the trend to smaller firms will result in

half the workforce being employed in firms of less than 50 people by 2000 (1996, p 134). It would be reasonable to expect the nature of learning at work to differ significantly between large, formalised organisations and smaller, less structured organisations.

The focus on such large organisations will allow Eraut to offer an important version of Michels' 'acid test' (Michels, 1982). Originally developed in the early 20th century by Michels to test the 'iron law of oligarchy' (that all organisations in time become hierarchical) the acid test sought to explore the hypothesis by studying the case where this was most *unlikely* to be true (a political party dedicated to popular power). Eraut's work enables us to explore whether, in organisations with highly developed formal training procedures, it is actually informal learning that matters, as Coffield's iceberg analogy suggests (see introductory chapter to this volume). However, we cannot assume that informal learning in such contexts represents informal learning in all contexts.

The unit of analysis sampled in Eraut's work, the individual worker, also presents a problem. The "focus was on employees at professional/managerial and technical/ supervisory levels (NVQ 3, 4, 5)" (Eraut et al, 1998a, p 3). His data shows that only 12.5% of the sample (15/120) did not hold qualifications at the level of Higher National Certificate (HNC), Higher National Diploma (HND), or above (Eraut et al, 1998a, p 9). These people were largely concentrated in the health sector where eight nursing assistants were sampled, a type of work which is being rapidly integrated into, and upgraded in, the National Vocational Qualification (NVQ) system. Such a sample is substantially unrepresentative of the working population as a whole. According to the National Advisory Council for Education and Training Targets (NACETT), in 1995 (as Eraut's sample was being drawn) only 41% of the workforce held qualifications of NVQ Level 3 or above (NACETT, 1996). Another version of Michels' acid test is thus possible (those studied are the workers whose status depends on formal qualifications, but in reality they gain the necessary knowledge through informal means). However, we cannot assume that informal learning for those at NVQ Levels 3, 4, 5 is the same as, for example, that for the 15-20% of Local

Enterprise Company Skillseekers classified as having Special Training Needs because they are not expected to reach Level 2 in two years without special intervention. In the context of a workforce polarising between the knowledge rich and a class of workers whose skills are being reduced to the 'generic skills' of functional literacy, conformity, punctuality and maximum productivity, a focus solely on the knowledge rich runs the risk of heightening the polarisation.

Second, the research method used by Eraut appears to pull the research away from its stated aims. Eraut expresses the need for methodological innovation in research on learning in employment (Eraut et al, 1998a, p 3) and concludes in Chapter 1 of this volume that "the problems faced by researchers investigating non-formal learning are considerable". He describes two major ways of conceptualising the relationship between propositional knowledge and knowledge-in-action:

One is to start from propositions and examine how they are differently transformed for use in different contexts ... the other is to start from knowledge-in-use in a particular context, situated knowledge, and examine ways in which it can be even partially described and the extent to which it can be represented in a form which gives it meaning across a wider range of contexts. (Eraut et al, 1998a, p 5)

Eraut also draws on the work of deJong who suggests three theoretical perspectives about on-the-job training: the detailed task analysis and social engineering of Human Performance Technology; the Learning Process Perspective of adult education; and Activity Theory of the social nature of learning and working (Eraut et al, 1998a, pp 7-8).

The method used was to conduct two interviews with the informants, the second being an extension of the first. The informant was sent a transcript of the first interview, and a list of questions for elaboration, prior to the second interview. The topics of the first interview were the 'what' and the 'how' of workplace learning. The topics of the second interview were the elaboration and further exploration of the first and the investigation of the factors affecting workplace learning (see Chapter 2). The design and conduct of these interviews are exemplary but the appropriateness of this method for the research questions asked must be questioned.

The thrust of Eraut's work is towards analysing knowledge-in-action through Learning Process and Activity Theory perspectives, but the method pulls back towards more decontextualised propositional knowledge and the Human Performance Technology perspective. Seeking understandings of deeply situated knowledge through interview is likely to foster responses from informants which are generalised and decontextualised. Hargreaves et al (1975) faced a similar problem in their classic study of school rules. Asking teachers in interview about school rules produced responses in terms of formal codes and it was only when they started from classroom observation, later asking teachers to 'fill in' what had been happening at specific moments, that the rules-in-action could be (re)constructed. It is not surprising that Eraut's research generates summaries that seem to fit better with a task analysis and social engineering perspective of Human Performance Technology perspective than with the desired Learning Process and Activity Theory perspectives:

Learning goals are identified which they pursue by a combination of self directed learning and taking advantage of relevant learning opportunities as and when they appear. (Eraut et al, 1998a, p 1)

Eraut did encourage "respondents to elaborate on salient learning episodes or to exemplify general statements about learning" (Eraut et al, 1998a, p 10), but these appear incidental to the main structure of the two interviews. In reflecting on the work, Eraut does recognise "the limitations of single or even double interviews for eliciting evidence of processes that, if not entirely tacit, do not readily come to mind" (Eraut et al, 1998a, p 11) and in Chapter 1 of this volume he suggests possible follow up research:

A prolonged period of fieldwork, perhaps two weeks in each participant's workplace, would have enabled us to gather much more evidence about workplace activities, decisions and transactions; and this would have then prompted many more questions about the learning which made their performance possible. (p 17)

While this autocritique shares many features with our position, Eraut does not propose the full methodological transition necessary for the ethnographic projects he suggests, seeing the analytic framework of the current study as transferable to the ethnographic studies.

The focus of our third critique is the analytic framework generated by Eraut's research. This sophisticated and systematic framework is in three domains (what is being learned; how it is being learned; and factors affecting learning). Within each of these there is an extensive taxonomy for the classification of the data. The analytic strategy is that of linking the three domains into quasi-causal statements. As such the research sits uneasily in the interstice between a formal positivism and a full ethnography. The pull of the framework is to statements about the conditions under which different types of learning occur through quasi-quantifying statements such as:"*most* of the knowledge classified as ... is acquired *mainly* by non-formal approaches" or "confidence was *frequently* cited by our respondents as both the *major* outcome of a *significant* learning experience and a *critical determinant* of good performance at work" (Eraut et al, 1988, pp 19, 27, emphasis added).

If research is to understand learning as a situated social practice then Eraut's approach of developing taxonomies and the search for quasi-quantifying generalisation tends to the static, and does not address the phenomena in conceptual terms consonant with their nature. In trying to address learning as a situated social practice we see much value in the overclaimed but underutilised phenomenological tradition.

Bracketing skills and informal learning

In order to explore the potential of the phenomenological tradition for understanding the nature of informal learning we want to focus on two of Schutz's essays: 'The stranger' (Schutz, 1976) and 'Common sense and scientific interpretation of human action' (Schutz, 1962). In 'The stranger' Schutz addresses the problem of how people may acquire the knowledge necessary to pass as a

competent member of a new social group. The cultural pattern of group life consists of:

> *... all the peculiar valuations, institutions, and systems of orientation and guidance (such as folkways, mores, laws, habits, customs, etiquette, fashions) which ... characterise, if not constitute, any social group at a given moment in its history. (Schutz, 1976, p 92)*

For Schutz this cultural pattern is characterised by incoherence, partiality and contradiction, an illogicality which derives its logic from culture being a working tool for making sense of the (incoherent) social world rather than a system designed, as it were, *de novo*:

> *It is a knowledge of trustworthy recipes for interpreting the social world and for handling things and men in order to obtain the best results in every situation with a minimum of effort by avoiding undesirable consequences. (Schutz, 1976, p 95)*

Schutz calls this the "natural attitude" – a complex series of assumptions, "just to be followed but not understood" (Schutz, 1976, p 104), which makes the social world manageable. These assumptions only come to consciousness when the flow of routine social business is interrupted by a crisis, the non-functioning of one or more of them.

The 'stranger' is a crisis incarnate, a person inserted into the social group who does not share its basic assumptions: "he becomes essentially the man who has to place in question nearly everything that seems to be unquestionable to the members of the approached group" (Schutz, 1976, p 96). For Schutz the 'stranger' is an objective observer of the culture of the group in the sense that she or he has consciously to acquire, and to interrelate, each element of the culture which, to members, is habitual, semi-conscious and automatic: the 'stranger' for Schutz has "a grievous clear-sightedness" (Schutz, 1976, p 104).

We want to take two major insights for *The Learning Society Programme* from this brief essay by Schutz. First, if we follow Schutz, the conceptualisation of the knowledge necessary to become a competent member of the workplace is radically extended. Formal, production oriented skills recede in importance (but do not disappear) while, foregrounded, are the cultural tenets which go to make up the 'natural attitude' of the workplace, the essential prerequisite for the competent performance of any of its task. In this sense the work of Eraut, still focused on production oriented skills, stops well short of the broader conceptualisation of knowledge necessary if we are to take the issue of what is learned informally at the ethnographic level he proposes.

Second, we suggest that the study of people with learning difficulties as workers represents an opportunity of wider significance to understand the nature of workplace competence. If we move away from a medical model of learning difficulties and into an attribution theory framework which treats the characteristics of people not as intrinsic, personal qualities but as traits attributed to them by others, then the classification, both formally and informally, of people as less than usually competent presents us with a spontaneous breach of the natural attitude of the workplace. The person with learning difficulties tends, by history, by biography and by social definition, to be a 'stranger' both to this 'natural attitude' and to the processes of its acquisition. In this sense studying the acculturation to work of people with learning difficulties offers a more 'objective' view of workplace knowledge and its acquisition than studying those for whom the process of acculturation is relatively unproblematic.

These two implications from 'The stranger' correspond to our first two critiques of the work of Eraut (of the research method; of the sample). If we turn to our third critique, that Eraut's analytic framework sits uneasily between being a 'positivist' classification system with quasi-quantitative generalisations and being an ethnographic account more consonant with the nature of the phenomenon being studied, then another essay by Schutz offers insights. In 'Common sense and scientific interpretation of human action' (1962) Schutz develops an ideal typical analysis through his idea of the 'homunculus', a theoretical model of a typical actor. This method draws from the German Idealist tradition, following Weber, where the researcher constructs models of the events analysed which highlight key characteristics and relationships but which do *not* claim to represent any particular case nor the average nor the typical. In Weber's seminal *The protestant ethic and the spirit of capitalism*

(1985) the angst-ridden protestant corresponds (so far as we know) to no early modern protestant but is a model by which to understand the economic and cultural dynamic of protestantism per se. Schutz ascribes to his 'homunculus':

> ... *a merely specious consciousness ... which is constructed in such a way that its presupposed stock of knowledge at hand ... would make actions originating from it subjectively understandable provided that these actions were performed by real actors within the social world.* (Schutz, 1962, p 41)

The analytic discipline on the homunculus is enshrined in three demands: that the knowledge ascribed to the model is logically consistent and can therefore explain the illogicality and incoherence observed in the actions of the social actors analysed; that the knowledge is such that the actions observed can be seen to be the consequence of that knowledge; and that the social action produced by the homunculus would allow it to pass as a competent member of the group.

Applying this type of explanation to people with learning difficulties trying to enter employment promises to generate models of the seen but not noticed conditions of competent workplace membership, conditions which otherwise would lie below the level of consciousness accessible through formal interviews. The homunculus promises a more processual account of implicit knowledge and how it is acquired than the classification scheme which Eraut generates. In the past decade supported employment projects have emerged in North America and Britain which attempt to acculturate people with learning difficulties into ordinary jobs in ordinary workplaces. Such projects represent a spontaneous 'bracketing' of the natural attitude to what it means to be a worker and thus an important opportunity for its analysis. It is to these which we now turn.

Supported employment, skills and informal learning

As suggested above, the introduction of a person with learning difficulties to the workplace can represent the introduction of 'spontaneous stranger' for whom some of the deeply implicit rules of competent membership of work have to be made explicit. In the past decade Britain has seen the significant growth of supported employment projects (from five in 1986 to 210 in 1995 [Beyer, 1997, p 7]) which aim to effect just such introductions. (These supported employment projects are different from the Employment Services' Supported Employment Programme by which an employer is paid a negotiated percentage of the wage of the disabled person as compensation for lost productivity. The two types of supported employment may interact. Some remarkable unintended consequences of the Employment Service Programme have come to light in our research but we do not focus on these here.) The history of these projects from their origins in North America to their current activity in Britain contains important general insights into the nature of workplace competence and its acquisition.

The move to supported employment projects began in the late 1970s in North America with action-research studies of a small number of people with learning difficulties maintaining employment in open labour market settings with ad hoc support. This initial phase focused on employment through the open labour market (especially with payment of the rate for the job) and the use of job coaches. Vacancies would be scanned and possible employment for people with learning difficulties identified. A person would be matched to the job and then a 'job coach' would enter the workplace ahead of the person with learning difficulties in order to learn the job. Once this was achieved the person with learning difficulties would take on the job with the support of the job coach who would gradually withdraw the support until the person with learning difficulties was doing the job effectively unaided, and only periodic monitoring visits were then necessary. In Eraut's terms this represents a circuit of routinisation by which the coach undertakes the implicit learning necessary for the job and makes this available as deliberative learning for the person with learning difficulties in order that it might become their implicit knowledge (see Chapter 1).

These American studies coincided with "an emerging behavioural technology" (Rusch and Hughes, 1990, p 6) which aimed to go beyond the analysis and reinforcement of behaviours directly related to the production process. The move to an "ecobehavioural"

approach sought to analyse and reinforce "the complex discriminations" needed to "address the varying expectations and demands of co-workers, supervisors and the supported employees themselves" (Rusch and Hughes, 1990, p 7).

*En*able, a major Scottish charity working with those with learning disabilities as part of the European Union *Inclusio* programme, defines workplace skills which the job coach will acquire and pass on to the person with learning difficulties thus:

> *This is so-called job analysis and nothing is left to chance. Not only do they learn the technical skills required, they will also check out other job-related routines – getting to work, keeping the uniform clean, signing-in etc. They also identify the 'workplace culture'. Are all the workers on first-name terms? Is it an unwritten rule that you don't tell on your workmates? (Enable, 1997, p 2)*

The field of 'ecobehaviourism' is littered with different and competing 'systems' of matching the person with job. 'Vocational Profiling' is perhaps the most common approach to the assessment of the capacity for employment of people with learning difficulties in the UK. The search for "ecological rather than predictive validity" (Mcloughlin, quoted in Beyer and Hill-Tout, 1996, p 15) results in a far-reaching assessment of the individual and of the workplace:

> *Many factors may affect the person's ability to do a job, not just their practical and cognitive skills. This may involve the assessor taking information from a wide range of sources, with the person's permission, which may include family friends, current and past professionals, and observations at home, in leisure, recreation.... When a potential job has been identified it is important to know as much as possible about that job and workplace as we know about the person who may be placed in the job. Here the key appears to be to look beyond the skills required for tasks of the job to questions of social and work culture for any job under consideration. (Beyer and Hill-Tout, 1996, pp 17-18)*

Two major implications for our understanding of 'what' is learned formally or informally may thus be drawn from a decade's experience of introducing 'strangers' into mainstream employment: the skills necessary for competent membership of the workforce extend far beyond those which are traditionally discussed in the 'knowledge and skills for employment' literature. Central to such an expanded notion of skill is the raft of cultural prerequisites for everyday work, the seen but noticed features of membership which may serve to include people in, or exclude people from, the workplace. This experience suggests that Eraut's engagement with the social relations of workplace learning, the concept of situated learning (see Chapter 1), is still too limited, being concerned with the social construction of task-oriented knowledge rather than these wider conditions for competent membership.

The second implication, a corollary of the first, is that the assessment and selection of people for membership of the workforce involves the surveillance not only of the cognitive/mechanical skills pertaining to the job but also, more importantly, of their cultural heritage. Perry and Beyer summarise their research on employer perceptions in South Wales:

> *Basic competencies in interpreting and manipulating numbers were felt to be important skills to have prior to taking up an entry level job. Basic communication was also rated most commonly as necessary prior to starting, the person being expected to be able to understand instructions, give information, ask for help and to know what to do in an emergency. Getting on with co-workers and supervisors was seen as a third important prerequisite, and looking clean and presentable a fourth. For the vast majority of skill groups, however, competency was seen as either not absolutely necessary or acquirable on the job. (Perry and Beyer, 1995, p 17, emphasis added)*

To date we have focused on the 'eco' of ecobehaviourism and now we must turn to its 'behaviourism': how what is learned is learned. The history of supported employment's attempts to train people with learning difficulties for work similarly illuminates the nature of learning to be a worker. 'Systematic instruction' was originally developed in the late 1960s by Gold in North America at a time when 'programmed instruction' had become almost an orthodoxy in industrial training (Field, 1996, p 345). 'Systematic Instruction' has since been taken up by supported employment projects particularly through the British marketing company, Merit

Employment Equity Ltd. It claims that it is used in 90% of supported employment projects and that Marks and Spencer in south London now use it for the induction of all new staff (Steele, 1994, p 15) – this chapter was first drafted before this example became even more pertinent.

Steele defines the key features of Systematic Instruction as a belief "that people with severe disabilities had much more potential than anyone realised; that all people with disabilities should have the same opportunities to live an ordinary life; that everyone can learn if we can work out how to teach them" (Steele, 1994, p 15). The 'working out' of 'how to teach them' has resulted in what Steele describes as a culturally normative teaching technology. This 'technology' consists of analysing the workplace (not a proxy) into the components of the required tasks, the setting up of a complex series of natural cues and reinforcements which lead the person with learning difficulties from component to component of each task, and from task to task. The scope of this complex scheduling is not only the production process but also "the company culture and employer and company expectations" (Steele, 1994, p 15) so "that appropriate dress codes, personal hygiene and social behaviour are reinforced" (Beyer, 1995, p 60).

The advocates of supported employment claim important success in enabling people with learning difficulties to take and retain open employment, achievements which are widely argued to be the key route to social integration. In 1995 Beyer, Goodere and Kilsby estimated that there were more than 5,000 people employed through such schemes, a significant number but still only a tiny percentage of the potential pool (Beyer et al, 1996, p 1). These jobs were concentrated in cleaning/domestic work, grounds keeping and assembly work.

A concern that people with learning difficulties often do not maintain their jobs runs through the literature on supported employment, despite the substantial claims made for the 'technology' of applied behaviour analysis. Chadsey-Rusch's review of the North American literature concludes that "there is ample evidence to suggest a major reason for job loss for persons with mental retardation may be their lack of social skills" (Chadsey-Rusch, 1992, p 405). Beyer's British survey suggests that "poor work behaviour ... and inappropriate social skills were common reasons given for job failure" (1997, p 11). Such findings reinforce the argument above that the cultural prerequisites of work are more important than specific task-related skills. These concerns have led to the development of 'natural supports' in supported employment, people who are not professionals in the learning difficulties field but who are already 'members' of the workplace who take on a responsibility, formally or informally, to teach and support the newcomer. The key focus of such natural supports is not the production process itself but the sharing of "essential and subtle knowledge" of the workplace culture (Beyer, 1995, p 66). It is just this order of subtle, cultural knowledge which behaviourism finds impossible to squeeze into its conceptual framework, as the contortions of Skinner's *Verbal behaviour* (1957) hilariously demonstrate. The problems of job loss through poor acculturation and the consequent shift to 'natural supports' implies that the behaviourism of ecobehaviourism is, at best, restricted to the second order issues of specific production performances or, more likely in our view, is simply wrong-headed.

The implications of the trajectory of supported employment in terms of the process of learning in a learning society are substantial. Given the centrality of the 'cultural' to work suggested above, the focus in the 'knowledge and skills for employment' literature on producing taxonomies of competencies, their components and their performance criteria is substantially mistaken; becoming a competent member of the workplace depends less on formally defined skills and their acquisition through training than on scarcely noticed processes of acculturation into social networks and their whole ways of life.

Conclusion: learning difficulties in a learning society

Studying implicit knowledge, particularly through the example of introducing people with learning difficulties into the routine workplace, redirects The Learning Society discourse in two dimensions: from a human capital frame of reference towards a social capital frame; from the dominance of utilitarian definitions of The Learning Society towards a humanistic definition.

Human capital perspectives on education and training have dominated theoretical and policy thinking for three decades as part of a systematic attempt by neo-classical economists to reduce all aspects of individual and social life to market choices (Fine and Green, forthcoming). Learning Society discourse bears the stamp of this context with an overwhelming emphasis on skills as human capital, a third factor of production along with physical and finance capital. The metaphor of 'capital' entails a focus on individuals (owners), formal training (investment), quantity (skill levels) and wages (rates of return). While there is an active aggregation by governments and international agencies of individuals into national economies, with differential performance being explained in terms of varying levels of human capital, the conceptual framework allows little or no space for production being a social process.

What Eraut's work on the acquisition of skills in the workplace points to is the need for understanding the networks of social relations through which workplace learning occurs and through which formally accredited human capital is put into action. What the experience of the supported employment of people with learning difficulties points to is the relatively minor role of the formal competencies understood as human capital in comparison with the seen but not noticed cultural prerequisites for competent workplace membership.

In recent years the concept of social capital has been taken from the work of Bourdieu, Coleman and Putnam to apprehend such phenomena. For Bourdieu social capital is the network of contacts which allow an elite to reproduce itself (Bourdieu and Passeron, 1977) and, in later work, it sits alongside a glittering array of other capitals, cultural, symbolic, linguistic and so on (Bourdieu, 1997). Coleman's work proletarianises the concept in its use to explain the statistically anomalous, high performance of children from relatively poor backgrounds in Catholic schools in the USA (Coleman, 1990). In this explanation social capital refers to the normative order shared between home and school. Coleman later (1994) installs social capital as the fourth term in multivariate economic equations alongside physical, financial and human capital in order to explain differential economic performance. Putnam (1993), in attempting to explain the differential success of the north and south of Italy, comes to an explanation in terms of social capital as forms of civil society. In documenting the perceived decline of social capital in the USA Putnam (1996) defines social capital in terms of shared networks, norms and trust. We will consider the implications of social capital understandings of The Learning Society once we have discussed the competing utilitarian and humanistic components of the working definition of The Learning Society used in the ESRC programme.

The working definition of a learning society in the research programme is:

A learning society would be one in which all citizens acquire a high quality general education, appropriate vocational training and a job (or series of jobs) worthy of a human being, while continuing to participate in education and training throughout their lives. A learning society would combine excellence with equity and would equip all its citizens with the knowledge, understandings and skills to ensure national economic prosperity and much more besides. The attraction of the term 'the learning society' lies in the implicit promise not only of economic development but the regeneration of our whole public sphere. Citizens of a learning society would, by means of their continuing education and training, be able to engage in critical dialogue and action to improve the quality of life of the whole community and to ensure social integration as well as economic success. To define the learning society in this way is to make clear the scale of the task facing the UK. (ESRC, 1994)

Such a definition is an admixture of two ingredients: a utilitarian emphasis on learning as an activity primarily directed at economic competitiveness; a humanistic emphasis on self-development, social solidarity and social justice. Such a combination is

an updated example of the familiar social democratic settlement of the 1960s (CCCS, 1981), education as the privileged site for combining social justice with economic efficiency. However, the four riders of The Learning Society (knowledge-skills-employment-competitiveness) gallop together in one direction, utilitarianism. The experience of people with learning difficulties in training systems suggests that the current pursuit of competitiveness is excluding more and more people from the labour market as having 'special needs' and that such exclusion limits lives and negates social solidarity (Baron et al, 1997, 1998b). Despite the attraction of the term 'Learning Society', there is little reason to believe that it resolves the tensions between its competing components any better than did Harold Wilson's vision of social division melting in the white heat of the technological revolution in the 1960s.

Using the two couplets (human and social capital, utilitarian and humanistic definitions) we can identify four ideal typical visions of a learning society (see Table 1).

We can imagine no *societal* vision based on Type 3, The Learning Society as liberal adult education. In contrast, Type 1, The Learning Society where each individual, as human capitalist, takes responsibility for their own investment in training and reaps any reward which the market offers is the dominant definition of The Learning Society. Eraut's work on knowledge at work shows that in the place where we might expect human capitalism to be strongest, the dynamics of knowledge creation and circulation are thoroughly social. Eraut's work suggests the need to redefine The Learning Society in a Type 2 manner, society as networks of cooperating individuals sharing knowledge to achieve some common purpose. This corresponds closely to the social vision of social capital theorists such as Fukuyama (1995). Central to this vision is the idea of shared goals, particularly a shared commitment to

Table 1: Ideal typical visions of a learning society

	Utilitarian	Humanistic
Human capital	1 Learning Society as personal upskilling	3 Learning Society as liberal adult education
Social capital	2 Learning Society as teamworking	4 Learning Society as social solidarity

the market competitiveness of the group, be it firm or nation. Such solidarity is highly conditional and depends on exclusion of any who have different goals or who are seen as less competitive. Our work in the ESRC Programme with people with learning difficulties in Scotland suggests the need for a Type 4 definition of The Learning Society as a society where social solidarity is both inclusive and pluralistic, with the acceptance, or celebration, of difference as a primary organising principle rather than profitability. The working definition of a learning society contains seven words which have yet to be explored in the ESRC Programme: what is 'a job worthy of a human being'?

References

Baron, S., Riddell, S. and Wilkinson, H. (1997) 'After Karaoke: adult education, learning difficulties and social renewal', *Scottish Journal of Adult and Continuing Education*, vol 4, no 2, pp 19-44.

Baron, S., Riddell, S. and Wilkinson, H. (1998b) 'The best burgers: the person with learning difficulties as worker', in T. Shakespeare (ed) *The disability reader: Social sciences perspectives*, London: Cassell.

Baron, S., Stalker, K., Wilkinson, H. and Riddell, S. (1998a) 'The learning society: the highest stage of human capitalism' in F. Coffield (ed) *Learning at work*, Bristol: The Policy Press, pp 49-59.

Beyer, S. (1995) 'Real jobs and supported employment', in T. Philpot and L. Ward (eds) *Values and vision: Changing ideas for services for people with learning disabilities*, London: Butterworth-Heinemann, pp 55-72.

Beyer, S. (1997) 'Supported employment in Britain', *Tizard Learning Disability Review*, vol 2, no 2, pp 6-14.

Beyer, S. and Hill-Tout, J. (1996) *Approaches to vocational assessment for people with learning disabilities*, Cardiff: Welsh Centre for Learning Disabilities, Applied Research Unit.

Beyer, S. and Kilsby, M. (1996) 'The future of employment for people with learning disabilities', *British Journal of Learning Disabilities*, vol 24, pp 134-7.

Beyer, S., Goodere, L. and Kilsby, M. (1996) *Costs and benefits of supported employment*, Cardiff: Welsh Centre for Learning Disabilities, Applied Research Unit.

Bourdieu, P. (1997) 'The forms of capital', in A.H. Halsey, H. Lauder, P. Brown and A. Stuart-Wells (eds) *Education: Culture, economy, society*, Oxford: Oxford University Press.

Bourdieu, P. and Passeron, J.-C. (1977) *Reproduction in education, culture and society*, London: Sage Publications.

CCCS (Centre for Contemporary Cultural Studies) (1981) *Unpopular education*, London: Hutchinson.

Chadsey-Rusch, J. (1992) 'Towards defining and measuring social skills in employment settings', *American Journal on Mental Retardation*, vol 96, no 4, pp 405-18.

Coleman, J. (1990) *Equality and achievement in education*, Boulder, CO: Westview Press.

Coleman, J. (1994) *Foundations of social theory*, Cambridge: Belknap Press.

Enable (1997) 'So just what is supported employment', *Newslink: Supported Employment Special*, Spring, p 2.

Eraut, M. (nd) *Skills, competence and transfer: Towards clarifying meanings and inferences; a new conceptual framework*, unpublished mimeograph, Brighton: Institute of Education, University of Sussex.

Eraut, M. (1994) *Developing professional knowledge and competence*, London: Falmer Press.

Eraut, M., Alderton, J., Boylan, A. and Wraight, A. (1995) *Learning to use scientific knowledge in education and practice*, London: English National Board for Nursing, Midwifery and Health Visiting.

Eraut, M., Alderton, J., Cole, G. and Senker, P. (1998) *Development of knowledge and skills in employment*, Brighton: University of Sussex Institute of Education.

ESRC (Economic and Social Research Council) (1994) *The Learning Society: Knowledge and skills for employment: Research Specification*, Swindon: ESRC.

Field, J. (1996) 'Learning for work: vocational education and training', in R. Fieldhouse (ed) *A history of modern British adult education*, Leicester: NIACE, pp 333-53.

Fine, B. and Green, F. (forthcoming) 'Economics and social capital', in S. Baron, J. Field and T. Schuller (eds) *Social capital: Critical perspectives*, Oxford: Oxford University Press (provisional title).

Fukuyama, F. (1995) *Trust: The social virtues and the creation of prosperity*, London: Hamish Hamilton.

Hargreaves, D., Hester, S. and Mellor, F. (1975) *Deviance in classrooms*, London: Routledge.

Michels, R. (1982) *Political parties*, Basingstoke: Macmillan.

NACETT (National Advisory Council for Education and Training Targets) (1996) *Skills for 2000: The UK's national targets for education and training*, London: NACETT.

Perry, J. and Beyer, S. (1995) '"Training pays" – but for who?', *Llais*, vol 35, Winter, pp 16-18.

Putnam, R. (1993) *Making democracy work: Civic tradition in modern Italy*, Princeton, NJ: Princeton University Press.

Putnam, R. (1996) 'Who killed civic America?', *Prospect*, March, pp 66-72.

Riddell, S., Wilson A. and Baron, S. (1999) 'Supported employment in Scotland', *Journal of Vocational Rehabilitation*, Special Issue on Supported Employment, vol 5, pp 57-70.

Rusch, F. and Hughes, C. (1990) 'Historical overview of supported employment', in F. Rusch (ed) *Supported employment: Models, methods and issues*, Sycamore, IL: Sycamore Publishing Company, pp 5-14.

Schutz, A. (1962) 'Common sense and scientific interpretation of human action', in M. Natanson (ed) *Alfred Schutz: Collected papers I; the problem of social reality*, The Hague: Martinus Nijhoff.

Schutz, A. (1976) 'The stranger', in A. Brodersen (ed) *Alfred Schutz: Collected papers II; studies in social theory*, The Hague: Martinus Nijhoff.

Skinner, B.F. (1957) *Verbal behaviour*, Englewood Cliffs, NJ: Prentice Hall.

Steele, D. (1994) 'How SI unlocks people's potential', *Community Living*, vol 7, no 4, p 15.

Weber, M. (1985) *The protestant ethic and the spirit of capitalism*, London: Routledge.

4

Formalising learning: the impact of accreditation

Pat Davies

Introduction

This paper arises from *The Learning Society Programme* project: 'The impact of credit-based systems of learning on learning cultures'. In the context of a widening and expanding system of qualifications, it seeks to map out: the shifting nature of what counts as learning in the public domain; the formalisation of informal learning; and the role of accreditation in that process. The definitions, explanations and evidence will draw on the work of the London Open College Network (LOCN) and the National Open College Network (NOCN) system of credit-based learning.

Context: the increasing significance of qualifications

The context for this examination of the changing characterisation of informal and formal learning is a wide and long-term pattern of change in the scope, scale and role of qualifications. Historically, qualifications have functioned as an exclusionary mechanism, selecting out the many and selecting in the few to a wide range of opportunities and possibilities. This function has now been undermined by three broad trends located in wider policy initiatives.

Firstly, the idea that to improve competitiveness in global markets, the level of skills in the labour force had to be raised and the proportion holding skills at all levels had to be improved, became the driving force of education and training policy in the late 1980s and early 1990s. Expectations about the capacity of young people and adults to improve their qualifications have been consequently revised and raised. It is illuminating to compare the most recent national target for 19-year-olds: 85% with Level 2 by the year 2002 (DfEE, 1999), with the view in the late 1950s and early 1960s that only the top 20% of young people were 'examinable' for O levels (Ainley, 1997).

Secondly, the development of the contract culture in the public sector – privatisation, marketisation and franchising – has been accompanied by an operational need to measure the capacity, the quality of service and the output of organisations. In education and training policy, qualifications have become the key measuring instrument not only of learners' achievement but also of the effectiveness of professionals and the performance of institutions. League tables, performance-related funding and performance-related pay all employ qualifications as a tool. Targets for the output of the whole education and training system are expressed in terms of qualifications. As the recent White Paper put it, "qualifications are a measure of success for both individuals and providers" (DfEE, 1999, para 5.22).

Thirdly, although rather more marginal at least in national policy discourse, there is the equity imperative which constructs qualifications as the key to addressing social exclusion, especially of young people and migrant groups. Recent reports in the UK (Kennedy, 1997; Dearing, 1996; NCIHE, 1997) have stated that qualifications and the development of 'small steps' towards qualifications should be the focus of approaches designed to widen access. The political agenda is the primary driving force of this, with economic considerations being secondary.

In general, the scope and scale of qualifications as a measure of formal learning have been extended, changing their role as a selection mechanism in the distribution of life chances. This process has been accompanied by a diversification of function that now includes the measurement of the education and training system as a whole as well as the actors and the learning within it.

Definitions and distinctions

It is important here to make clear a number of definitions and distinctions: between formal, non-formal and informal learning, between education and learning and between qualifications and accreditation.

The terms formal, non-formal and informal learning are problematic since their usage varies in different contexts. For example, Eraut et al (1998, p 6) have proposed that non-formal learning is that "which is not constrained (or supported by) prescribed frameworks", in particular, curriculum or qualifications frameworks. This definition could encompass training courses organised and delivered by the employer in the workplace but not linked to any externally recognised vocational qualifications. However, in the setting of a community project such activity might be viewed as formal provision on the basis of its mode of delivery. The idea of informal learning is a broad, loose and variable concept (McGivney, 1999) even within one setting. It is more useful for the purpose of this chapter to focus on the various dimensions that comprise the formal–informal spectrum rather than on the elaboration of very precise definitions. There are three dimensions relevant to our research study: the framework of curriculum and qualifications, intentionality, and the setting in which the learning takes place:

- The framework of curriculum and qualifications prescribes content and assessment arrangements and is strongly associated with a particular mode of delivery. Informal learning here is characterised by a negotiated, flexible agenda for learning, by group work and oral rather than

written communication and perhaps most importantly, by an absence of formal assessment of any type. It is also often underpinned by a philosophy of social learning and community development rather than individual advancement. As Eraut et al (1998) point out, it is 'adult education' contrasted to formal education and training.

- Some informal learning takes place in the 'life environment' (McGivney, 1999); it is experiential and usually unplanned by the learner. Learning may be unplanned by the learner but will be an important element of the intentions of the provider or agency. In academic programmes, for example, skills development may be submerged beneath a formal discipline-based curriculum or in youth work and community settings beneath the explicit agenda of resolving a personal, domestic or financial problem.

- The setting in which learning takes place is associated with its informality. McGivney (1999) refers to formal learning as that which takes place inside, and informal learning as that which takes place outside, a 'dedicated learning environment'. In our research study for *The Learning Society Programme*, we used detailed case studies in further education colleges (clear examples of the formal category) but also examined the impact of accreditation in organisations dedicated primarily to purposes other than learning: the workplace, prisons, trades unions, voluntary sector organisations, and community projects.

Credits, certificates and qualifications are part of a system of education rather than of learning per se. Jarvis (1997, p 175) made a distinction between education which is "a public phenomenon and provides public recognition for the learning it provides" and learning as "a private activity". Through the education system, learning is brought into the public domain for assessment and accorded recognition by the award of credits or of a qualification. Once rendered public in this form, learning can be represented to a third party (Wilson, 1999) and it has a use and exchange value (Fuller, 1995) for the individual.

There is a difference between qualifications and accredited learning: the former have a status, currency and legitimacy that the latter may not have. The latter includes certificates, awards or credits that are often 'small steps' towards greater involvement in education and training and may lead to qualifications (Kennedy, 1997). Similarly, qualifications may include, or may be entirely composed of, accredited units, but this is not necessarily the case; most traditional academic qualifications are not of this type. There is no clear official definition of a qualification, and as Ward (1996) pointed out, the terminology is very confusing. At sub-degree level, the Further Education Funding Council (FEFC) makes a distinction in the funding formula between programmes which lead to qualifications and those which do not ('Schedule 2' and 'non-Schedule 2' respectively). The important point for the purposes of this chapter is that programmes accredited by LOCN may be in either category. At the time of writing these definitions are under review by the Qualifications and Curriculum Authority (QCA) charged with developing a National Framework of Qualifications (QCA, 1999), and in 'Working Draft' form only. The White Paper (DfEE, 1999) has proposed changes in principle but how these will be operationalised and the precise timetable for doing so are not yet clear.

Formalising 'adult education'

[Quotations used in this part of the paper are drawn from interview data with learners and tutors as indicated. The setting was further education, unless stated otherwise.]

The concerns

The OCN system of credit-based learning had its roots in adult education and in a radical approach to adult learning (Davies, 1999a) intended to empower disadvantaged groups. Up until the mid-1990s it had developed steadily but slowly but was then given a major boost by changes in the Further Education Funding Council (FEFC) policy that required all programmes to be accredited and to offer progression in order to qualify for funding. At the time, the adult education budgets of the local education authorities (LEAs) were severely constrained, with many of them struggling to meet their statutory obligations, and the FE colleges were under increasing financial pressure to expand and widen participation. The funding was critical not only for existing provision but for the new programmes necessary to meet the expansion targets. The alternative of full cost fees was not a viable option, particularly for those courses aimed at socially excluded groups, and this was also opposed by many tutors on political grounds. Economic necessity was a major factor in the spread of LOCN accreditation and the increase in the number of learners registered (Davies, 1999b). However, this same factor tended to reinforce fears on the part of some tutors that accreditation threatened the 'informality' of their practice, echoing the debates around the kitemarking of access courses in the late 1980s (Davies and Parry, 1993).

There were fears concerning the introduction of assessment, which was required for accreditation. Most adult education provision quite deliberately involved no assessment, partly because tutors and managers believed that learners did not want it (see, for example, University of Cambridge, 1995; Cooke et al, 1996). More significant for the tutors and colleges who wanted to widen as well as expand participation, was the belief that fear of assessment was a demotivating factor among traditionally non-participating groups: "we are just constructing more and more hurdles for people to jump over". In addition, they feared that assessment would distort the purpose of the course: 'writing and filing' would be assigned a disproportionate importance at the expense of building self-confidence. Tutors also thought that they would be forced away from "being a facilitator and a resource into a more judgmental role – more like a traditional teacher".

The NOCN argued that assessment was never forced on learners; it was always voluntary and could be presented in a non-threatening way. If appropriate and diverse assessment techniques were employed, self-confidence could be enhanced rather than undermined and a culture of achievement promoted. It also stressed that the absence of any form of public recognition was itself exclusionary (see for example, Wilson, 1998). One tutor expressed it as a challenge: "Let all those people in this room who think qualifications are not important throw away their own". Nevertheless, the sense that accreditation might be perceived as a barrier was a strong one.

A second strand that we identified was most clearly illustrated in, but not exclusive to, the debates which took place in the trade union movement (Capizzi, 1999). Here a primary concern was that the form of accreditation should enable the unions to retain ownership and control of the programmes in order to sustain the value system that underpinned the curriculum. In particular, the commitment to a social, collaborative mode of learning and collective group development should not be replaced by an individualised or competitive culture.

There was also an anxiety that accreditation would constrain the student-centredness, not only of the content of the programmes but also of the teaching and learning methods, the style of teaching and the flexibility to change focus and 'go off at a tangent' if and when this was appropriate. This is not only a practical educational issue about "starting where the learners are" and "using their life experiences as a vehicle for learning", phrases used repeatedly by the tutors interviewed in our study, but is a core construct of practitioners in this field; it goes to the heart of what it is to be an adult educator (Hillier, 1998). Much of the language involved in the implementation of programmes based on 'learning outcomes' and the 'unitisation' arrangements was seen as being full of 'mechanical images' and the 'vocabulary of control' (Griffiths, 1994, p 122) rather than being used to emphasise the importance and value of the learning process itself and the collective experience of change and development.

One of the lines of enquiry in our research was to explore these concerns from the tutors' and learners' perspectives and to investigate the extent to which these dimensions of informality had been distorted by the process of accreditation.

The outcomes

Among management and teaching staff in FE (where much of the LEA adult education provision in London is located), the responses were blurred by the changes brought about by incorporation, mastering the new funding mechanism, following its subtle and not-so-subtle changes and dealing with the pressures on budgets. Particularly in the case study college where the credit-based curriculum was newly introduced (Capizzi et al, 1998), the reactions were mixed. Most of the tutors (including those on the trade union courses) located their professional identity in terms of their students – for example, "I work with refugees", rather than in terms of a discipline, a qualification or an occupational area. What they saw as important was the 'bottom-up' approach to accreditation. This had given them the opportunity to continue pursuing their objectives "Having written most of the units ourselves ... we've written them to achieve the sort of things we want the students to achieve", and to embed their values – "you can give worth to those areas of education which otherwise students wouldn't get credit for".

Their perceptions of the value in practice of rewarding 'small steps' of achievement (Kennedy, 1997) were mixed. For some, the system worked as intended: "It gives people a sense that they're getting something and that they're going somewhere ... and ... if they're achieving it's really wonderful – it snowballs". Others found that it created "too many hurdles" and that "the students feel under constant pressure ... the first credits are awarded very early". It was reported that some students were "obsessed with levels" which seemed to operate as a proxy for marks and detracted from the process of learning: "Students do tend to focus on credit rather than on what they're doing and at the end of it, if you say to them what have you done, the answer is – I've got a credit". Several of the tutors reported that not only they, but also their students, had lost control of the programme: they were driven by the need to 'tick boxes'. However, others suggested that the tutors' control over the learning had been strengthened rather than diminished. Many tutors (especially those in the TUC programmes) emphasised that there was enough flexibility in the Open College system to enable them to be responsive to the needs of the students: "you would have to be pretty dim not to be able to manage to adapt activities to fit students' interests and the assessment criteria". The continued existence of the informal characteristics of the learners' experience was largely dependent on the ability and readiness of tutors to exploit the potential offered by the accreditation arrangements and some did so more than others (Capizzi et al, 1998).

The tutors were clearly comparing the difference between their practice immediately before and after accreditation. However, for the learners the comparison was between their current experience and their previous encounter with the education system, which was frequently school, in the not so recent past. The overwhelming majority were more positive about the experience as an adult than as a young person and, as one learner put it, found it exciting "to discover how much I know". Among the minority who knew about accreditation before they began, some were initially worried that it might imply a traditional assessment regime as the sole determinant of success. Such anxieties seem to have been quickly dispelled and, in general, learners did not suggest that the forms of assessment introduced for accreditation had distorted the informal characteristics of the learning experience which they most appreciated. They pointed to features of their courses that echoed the characteristics of adult education valued by tutors: the absence of formal examinations, the variety of assessment techniques which were not "daunting" or "too pressured" and in particular they valued continuous assessment: "It helps to know you're gaining rather than leaving it to the last moment, with an exam".

They nevertheless valued certification: "Having a piece of paper to show you've done it". Despite the voluntary principle, most learners did submit their work for assessment, with around 67% awarded credit. Interestingly, in the case of the TUC programmes where the optional nature of 'going for the credit' was particularly emphasised by tutors, it was nevertheless taken up and successfully completed by almost all those registered on the programme. Most reported that for them the assessment had enhanced rather than diminished the value of the learning. Partly this was because the assessment methods were simply following activities they would undertake in any case – "because you don't realise you're taking it in and it lasts a lot longer than exams". Assessment gave these activities additional, valued, significance. Several mentioned, for example, the value of producing something 'concrete' – a file or a learning journal – which, while serving an assessment purpose, remained useful or stimulating at a personal level and was something to which they would return. This 'product' was not seen as 'alienated labour' for the consumption of the assessor, but rather something that they should do or would have liked to do on

other courses to enhance and consolidate their learning but "somehow you just don't do it".

Many learners pointed to the importance of the informal group, "group talking which at the end of the day gives you skills not learned in college". This was not only a vehicle for learning but also a source of solidarity and confidence. Learners in all the settings we investigated (including the French case study) talked of "being in it together" and all being "in the same boat". They referred to a personal relationship with the tutor, of a "language of equals" between them, a sense of "being on the same level", of feeling "like an adult rather than a kid", and of "a relaxed atmosphere with no rigid timetable forced on us".

Our study found no evidence that the formalisation of learning through the introduction of assessment had significantly undermined the informal dimensions of adult education or distorted the learning experience of the participants (a finding similar to that of studies of accreditation in other settings, see University of Cambridge, 1995; Cooke et al, 1996).

Formalising experience and implicit learning

One of the claims for a credit-based system of learning was that it would eliminate 'time-serving' since informal learning could be formally recognised for access to qualifications or for credit within programmes leading to qualifications, through the accreditation of prior experiential learning (APEL) (see for example, Robertson, 1994). In some contexts modularity has been sufficient to facilitate formal APEL arrangements, the modular degree programmes in the post-1992 universities are the most obvious example of this development. In our study, the arrangements in the Nord-Pas de Calais region of France where the system is more akin to a modular than to a credit-based system, were also promoting APEL (Davies, 1999a; Davies et al, 1997), although this was supported by legislation and specific finance. However, there was little evidence that APEL was being used in the LOCN system, particularly at lower levels. In part this related to the perceived high cost of the one-to-one work necessary to formalise APEL arrangements, but our analysis suggested that other factors were more significant. As indicated above, an important element of the professional identity of tutors was the group characteristics of 'their' students: refugees, ethnic minorities, working-class women or other disadvantaged learners. They operated with a strong social model of learning: the idea of the group or the community lay at the heart of their professional practice and their analysis of how disadvantage could and should be overcome. However, this commitment militated against the idea of APEL since that promoted individual rather than collective empowerment and recognised learning that had occurred outside the framework organised for achieving group learning. Some tutors in FE still located their professional identity more closely in their subject, although these represented a declining number: "People who came in saying, 'Oh I'm a psychologist' or 'I'm a mathematician', are now finding out that they're doing a much wider variety of things because that's what FE is about". Nevertheless, such tutors had a strong belief in their students' need to master the content of the curriculum, which implied an important role for the teacher. This too militated against an interest in the development of APEL arrangements.

Two other trends have promoted the formalisation of learning. Firstly, a great deal of learning in schools, colleges and universities was historically 'caught not taught'. A wide range of approaches to learning, social attitudes, interpersonal skills, teamwork, and group skills were conveyed either by the 'hidden curriculum' or developed through the teaching style. Similarly, spelling and different styles of writing (especially at higher education level) were developed indirectly through other subjects rather than being addressed or assessed directly. The development of these skills and attributes was located in the personal domain rather than the public and, although usually set within a prescribed curriculum framework, were put within a framework designed primarily to teach disciplinary knowledge. In the last decade there has been a major shift towards not only making such learning explicit but in formally teaching and assessing such skills, attributes and even ways of behaving. Alongside core and key skills in the universities and in NVQs, the Open Colleges have been very active in this area. LOCN has accredited programmes in 'career planning', 'communication skills', 'personal

development' and 'personal preparation', 'job preparation' and 'numeracy development'. Credits have been awarded in Access programmes for the application to higher education, and within Access to Teacher Training for professional ways of behaving, for example, punctuality and interaction with colleagues. Hence accreditation at all levels, from basic education to degrees, has made explicit and brought within the scope of assessment and thus into the public domain, a whole range of personal and interpersonal skills and attributes which were previously hidden beneath the formal prescribed frameworks.

The second trend relates to coherence. Traditionally, the coherence of a 'course' derived from theories and methodologies attached to a field of study, a discipline or a professional/vocational domain. However, NVQs have extended this to include a set of learning outcomes and competences, with a coherence derived from an occupational sector and functional roles. All these understandings of coherence imply a particular form of prescribed framework that is external to the individual. It was one of the tenets of the OCN system of credits (see, for example, Wilson, 1994) and of credit accumulation and transfer schemes generally (Robertson, 1994) that 'credit' offers a means to construct a definition of coherence rooted in the personal or professional needs and aspirations of the individual and thus be internally rather than externally defined and inscribed rather than prescribed. Despite formal statements in college documents and prospectuses, our study found little evidence that such individualisation had occurred in practice. Most learners who registered for credit with LOCN at Entry Level and Level 1 followed 'courses' defined by others. At Levels 2 and 3, there tended to be a greater range of choices available to learners and greater choice exercised by them. For example, there were Access Courses that included combinations of modules and units from across the whole college and could involve other organisations, such as theatres or community projects, so that learners were able to put together packages in many different ways. However, these options were frequently severely constrained in practice by timetables, rooms, teaching staff, or resources so that most learners continued to describe their experience as part of a cohort of students on a course rather than as an individualised activity. In

France, despite the constraints of a 'diplôme national' (Davies, 1999a) and the absence of many of the features of the OCN credit-based system, there was considerable variation between the programmes of the participants and they tended to be more closely linked to the employment of the individual.

Beyond education and training institutions

There has been a growing recognition that the learning which goes in formal institutions of education and training is only a small part of the totality of significant learning. At the forefront of this has been increased attention to the learning that occurs in the workplace. In *The Learning Society Programme*, for example, Eraut et al (1998) have suggested that much of the significant learning at work is brought about not by the education and training department of the organisation but through the operation of the micro-culture. The comparative dimension of our project has highlighted a similar growing interest among French researchers (see, for example, Barbier et al, 1996) in the way in which that micro-culture can be manipulated to maximise the learning of employees. Such processes are often managed by the production or the human resource manager rather than trainers and are usually a feature of learning organisations (Burgoyne et al, 1994) or routine learning in the professions (Gear et al, 1994). Just as there have been attempts for some time to imbue education and training with an enterprise culture (see, for example, CRAC/NICEC, 1986), private enterprise is also now being colonised by a learning culture, and the definition of what counts as learning is being extended to include more informal modes. Similarly, the in-house training programmes provided by employers, which have historically been completely separate from the prescribed frameworks of academic or vocational qualifications, are increasingly designed to articulate with, or even to form part of, external systems, especially NVQs.

In principle, the OCN system was ideally suited to capture informal learning in the workplace but in the London area this has not happened. The one case which existed is an exemplar of the use of accreditation to serve strategic management purposes and to provide progression opportunities for unqualified staff "at the bottom of the heap" (Davies, 1999b). However, it remains the only case, despite considerable promotion by the Training and Enterprise Council (TEC) and other London groupings of employers and education institutions. This cannot be explained by the reluctance of tutors in the colleges or in adult education since there was no requirement that they be involved. Although our study was limited in terms of fieldwork among employers not involved with LOCN, our evidence suggested that the financial incentives for using NVQs were significant. Where no NVQ existed and/or among employees with low levels of skills, there was little interest in promoting qualifications among employees.

Similar developments were taking place in the voluntary sector. As suggested above, qualifications have become increasingly important for professionals managing organisations. Certification has offered managers a useful tool to enhance the commitment of the volunteers to organisational values, to promote their learning and to publicly recognise their contribution and their skills, especially when the volunteers are themselves potential or ex-clients of the service. The OCNs have been active in this area. Accreditation was used to provide access to further training and/or to qualifications, particularly for those volunteers who were themselves members of excluded groups (for example, Asian women, young ex-offenders, or young unemployed people on environmental schemes). A number of programmes which included volunteers were approved, often combining linguistic skills with some training in advocacy, such as Community Interpreting and Bilingual Health Advocacy; there were also projects targeted at volunteers working with people with learning disabilities or their families (Heycock, 1997). Accreditation contributed to the formalisation of informal learning occurring at several levels in this context: the professional, the volunteer and the client.

A small part of our research also investigated the use of credit-based systems of learning in prisons, where the primary purpose of the organisation is control rather than learning. Formal education in prisons has traditionally led to qualifications of, for example, Pitman's and the Royal Society of Arts (RSA).

However, following recommendations from the Prison Service's own Education and Training Advisory Service (ETAS), there were limited moves to accredit, through the Open College system, programmes which previously involved no formal assessment. LOCN, for example, accredited programmes in Brixton, Pentonville and Wormwood Scrubs prisons in London, but the overall picture remained varied. On the one hand, there was some limited NVQ accreditation of catering skills demonstrated in the prison kitchens and, in some institutions, of gym programmes; on the other hand, the large amount of personal development in relation to drug and alcohol abuse, anger management or personal relationships remained unaccredited. Such activities are provided in prescribed frameworks 'owned' by psychologists, the probation service and increasingly prison officers, reinforced by administrative and departmental boundaries; the programmes were not accredited because they were not under the control of the education service (Carter, 1999). Although in the workplace the idea (if not necessarily the practice) of a learning organisation has become widespread, this was not the case in the prisons involved in our study. Interest in learning, especially in terms of changing behaviour, was commonplace but it did not seem to be a sufficiently powerful motivator to overcome the strength and territorial imperiousness of the various professional and departmental interests.

Conclusions

The growth of the NOCN as an awarding body for adult learning has contributed to the formalisation of learning, but the impact has varied in different settings and organisations. In further and adult education, although some tutors remained unconvinced, the majority believed that the informal elements of their practice had been improved or at least not distorted by accreditation. Learners, although using a different comparative frame, largely confirmed this picture and valued similar elements of the learning experience. Although they took certification for granted (unlike the tutors), this was dependent on the absence of formal examinations and a diversity of assessment methods. The formalisation of a large volume of existing and new 'adult education' through

accreditation and the inclusion of assessment does not appear to have undermined its informal characteristics. The system was used by tutors to assess and award credit formally for a wide range of individual and group skills previously submerged in academic and vocational programmes.

However, embedded in the same value system that sustained aspects of informality in the process of formalisation were elements that limited the impact of accreditation. Although resource constraints played a part, more important was the strong commitment to a social model of learning, which inhibited both the accreditation of prior experiential learning for individuals and the widespread development of highly individualised programmes of study.

Outside the institutions of education and training, the OCN system had a varied impact. In the workplace and prisons, informal learning was not being formalised through accreditation to any significant degree, although interesting examples existed. However, in trade union programmes a large and rapidly growing number of learners were awarded credit. In the voluntary sector and community projects, the development was embryonic but all the indications were that with appropriate resourcing the numbers would increase.

In general, the OCN credit-based system was more successful in formalising learning where the staff had a commitment to an equity agenda which was matched by organisational objectives; it had less impact where the professionals and the organisations had quite different primary purposes.

Acknowledgements

The author wishes to thank Liz Rees of the TUC for permission to use data obtained from work commissioned by them and Elaine Capizzi, Julia Carter and Tamsin Heycock of City University, who carried out most of the fieldwork and commented usefully on earlier drafts of this paper.

References

Ainley, P. (1997) 'Towards a learning or a certified society?', *Youth and Policy*, no 56, pp 4-13.

Barbier, J.M., Berton, F. and Boru, J.J. (1996) *Situations de travail et de formation*, Paris: L'Harmattan.

Burgoyne, J., Pedler, M. and Boydell (eds) (1994) *Towards the learning company: Concepts and practices*, Maidenhead: McGraw Hill.

Capizzi, E. (1999) *Learning that works: Accrediting the TUC programmes*, Leicester: National Institute of Adult Continuing Education.

Capizzi, E., Carter, J. and Davies, P. (1998) 'Making sense of credit: FE staff managing change', *Journal of Access and Credit Studies*, vol 1, no 1, pp 40-52.

Carter, J. (1999) 'Inside information', *Adults Learning*, vol 10, no 9, pp 19-21.

Careers Research and Advisory Council (CRAC)/ National Institute of Adult Continuing Education (NICEC) (1986) *Enterprise – a learning culture?*, Conference Report, Cambridge: CRAC.

Cooke, A., Mackle, K. and Sporing, M. (1996) '"Sleeping at the back" – student attitudes towards accreditation', *Scottish Journal of Adult and Continuing Education*, vol 2, no 1, pp 25-42.

Davies, P. (1999a) 'Inclusion and exclusion: credits and *unités capitalisables* compared', in F. Coffield (ed) '*Why's the beer always stronger up North?*': *Studies of lifelong learning in Europe*, Bristol: The Policy Press.

Davies, P. '(1999b) 'A new learning culture? Possibilities and contradictions in accreditation', *Studies in the Education of Adults*, vol 30, no 3, pp 10-20.

Davies, P. and Parry, G. (1993) *Recognising access*, Leicester: NIACE.

Davies, P., Gallacher, J. and Reeve, F. (1997) 'The accreditation of prior learning: a comparison of current practice in the UK and France', *International Journal of University Adult Education*, vol 36, no 2, pp 1-21.

Dearing, Sir R. (1996) *Review of qualifications for 16-19 year olds*, London: Schools Curriculum and Assessment Authority.

DfEE (Department for Education and Employment) (1999) *Learning to succeed – A new framework for post-16 learning*, Cm 4392, London: The Stationery Office.

Eraut, M., Alderton, J., Cole, G. and Senker, P. (1998) *Development of knowledge and skills in employment*, Final Report of ESRC Project, Brighton: University of Sussex.

Fuller, A. (1995) 'Purpose, value and competence: contextualising competence based assessment', *British Journal of Education and Work*, vol 8, no 2, pp 60-77.

Gear, J., McIntosh, A. and Squires, G. (1994) *Informal learning in the professions*, Hull: School of Education, University of Hull.

Griffiths, M. (1994) 'Credit-based developments in Wales', *Journal of Access Studies*, vol 9, no 1, pp 115-23.

Heycock, T. (1997) *Voluntary organisations, training and credit*, Working Paper 3/5 for Project Advisory Forum, July: City University, London.

Hillier, Y. (1998) 'Informal practitioner theory: eliciting the implicit', *Studies in the Education of Adults*, vol 30, no 1, pp 35-52.

Jarvis, P. (1997) 'The paradoxes of the Learning Society', in J. Holford, C. Griffith and P. Jarvis (eds) *Lifelong learning: Reality, rhetoric and public policy*, Conference Proceedings, Guildford: University of Surrey.

Kennedy, H. (1997) *Learning works: Widening participation in further education*, Coventry: Further Education Funding Council.

McGivney, V. (1999) *Informal learning in the community: A trigger for change and development*, Leicester: NIACE.

NCIHE (National Committee of Inquiry into Higher Education) (1997) *Higher education in the learning society. Main Report*, London: NCIHE.

QCA (Qualifications and Curriculum Authority) (1999) *Consultation on flexibility within the national framework of qualifications*, London: QCA.

Robertson, D. (1994) *Choosing to change: Extending access, choice and mobility in higher education,* London: Higher Education Quality Council.

University of Cambridge (1995) *Credit where it's due,* Project Report, Employment Department Credit Frameworks and Learning Outcomes Programme, Cambridge: Department of Continuing Education, University of Cambridge.

Wilson, P. (1994) 'Access to higher education and credit accumulation and transfer: option or necessity?', *Journal of Access Studies,* vol 9, no 1, pp 10-23.

Wilson, P. (1998) 'Inclusion, entitlement and qualifications reform', *Adults Learning,* vol 9, no 7, pp 8-9.

Wilson, P. (1999) *Lifelong qualifications. Developing qualifications to support lifelong learners,* Leicester: NIACE.

5

Necessary and unnecessary learning: the acquisition of knowledge and 'skills' in and outside employment in South Wales in the 20th century

Ralph Fevre, Stephen Gorard and Gareth Rees

Introduction

There has been little research into learning that does not take the form of institutionalised, accredited participation in formal education or training. The sociology of education tradition usually emphasises an individual's formal rather than 'real' level of education (Girod, 1990), and there are sound methodological and philosophical reasons for this. Informal learning does not lead to such convenient measures as participation and pass rates, for example, and once its existence has been acknowledged it is more difficult to find an operational definition of learning on the continuum leading to the trivial and the commonplace (Coffield, 1997). Nevertheless, by effectively ignoring informal learning, writers may become confused over trends in skill formation over time (Gallie, 1988). There is also little evidence that indicators such as participation and qualifications are good predictors either of a person's value for employers or to society (Eraut, 1997). There is a danger that discourse concerning The Learning Society will be dominated by the providers, and become the empire of the 'schoolers' (Gorard et al, 1997b) or the adult educators.

This chapter uses a fairly broad definition of informal learning (not encompassed by the learning trajectories the present authors have discussed to date – see Gorard et al, 1998a), which covers learning at work and at leisure. Eraut (1997) has argued that if learning is defined as a "change in a person's capability or understanding", then it can encompass informal 'background' learning at work without also including all changes in behaviour. One of the purposes of this chapter is to examine the possibility of extending this use of the term learning to activities outside work.

From Eraut we gather that a great deal of learning goes on in work which is virtually unnoticed by researchers and even by employers but which is necessary to the organisations people work for (and perhaps also to the fulfilment of the individuals concerned) even though it is not acquired in any formal manner. In some cases the acquisition of this learning is an active process, and it does not do justice to this type of learning to describe it as coming about from 'sitting next to Nelly' (that type of informal training in which new recruits learn to do their jobs by watching an established employee at work). Eraut describes the informal learning being acquired by proactive individuals who seek out Nellies and others like her. These people adopt a variety of other methods in order to do their jobs and sometimes they transform those jobs in the process. The most active informal learners are in a process of constant transformation, both of themselves and of what they do. It is almost as if the best type of learning – and not simply that very basic learning without which the organisation could not function – is the informal type.

In many important respects we would seek to support and amplify this view on the basis of our research. We too think that the role of informal learning has been neglected; that there is much to be gained (for example, in terms of delineating lifelong learning and The Learning Society) from looking at those individuals who actively set about picking up all types of knowledge and competences; and that some of the most interesting types of learning are transformative (of selves and/or organisations). (The transformation of selves need not simply entail the individual becoming a more productive or creative employee, for example. In this case the acquisition of knowledge may be directly related to the acquisition of power in the workplace.) We are also interested in the balance between formal and informal learning in the workplace and in the relationship between both types of learning and the acquisition of the knowledge and competences necessary to the performance of particular jobs. We also have our own special interests to bring to bear on this topic including an interest in informal learning outside work and in the investigation of patterns of historical change. It is with this historical interest that our substantive discussion begins but we will, firstly, summarise our research project.

For the full background to this substantial project, and for detailed discussion of the methods of data collection and analysis used, see Rees et al (1997) and Fevre et al (1999). For a discussion of the theoretical basis of the study see Gorard et al (1997a) and for a presentation of the methods used see Gorard et al (1997b). In summary, the research was funded by the ESRC (Grant No L123251041) as part of *The Learning Society Programme*. Industrial South Wales is used as the focus of the study. It is regionally focused to allow the researchers to gain clear descriptions of the changing structures of objective opportunities for participation in education and training during the past 100 years. This has been achieved primarily by analysis of taped oral histories of families dating back to 1890 in the South Wales Coalfield Archive, by interviews with key participants with long experience in local

training, by secondary data analysis, and th experiences of the researchers in previous based studies. Within the focus area, a syste stratified sample of 1,104 education and training histories have been collected from respondents aged 15 to 65, identified from the electoral register. The second wave involved interviewing many of the children of those in the first wave, while the third wave collected unstructured narratives via in-depth re-interviews of 10% of those in the first two waves. These are the forms of evidence used to consider the changing prevalence of informal learning in South Wales. (The archive material draws very closely on Burge et al [1998], the majority of the key informant interviews were reported by Paul Chambers, and the qualitative analysis of the survey data was conducted by Emma Renold.)

Formal and informal learning in the workplace

The coalfield history discussed here and later in the chapter is derived from published memoirs and unpublished oral history data collected in the South Wales Miners Library and selected by Burge et al (1998). A century ago the Director of Mining Education for Glamorgan had concluded that:

"... the great bulk of our future colliers enter upon their calling with little or no knowledge of the mine. Educationalists, mining inspectors and engineers, managers, colliery proprietors, and the most capable leaders amongst the colliers themselves, have all bewailed the lack of suitable preparatory instruction."

However, this did not mean that the thousands of new recruits to coal-mining in South Wales in the later 19th and early 20th century had no instruction. In fact, they were trained in a completely informal system which relied on experienced miners to pass on their knowledge and skills to new recruits. For the purposes of this chapter, the most important point to grasp is that it is very difficult to see how such knowledge and skills could have been imparted in a more formal manner. As the following discussion illustrates, the skills and knowledge involved were immensely impressive (and vital – to a miner's health and safety, for example), but they were not the sort of skills and knowledge that a formal, standardised system of training could handle successfully.

Each new recruit to the industry was allocated to a work partner (or what would now be called a mentor) upon whom he was completely dependent at this early stage. The mentor helped the new collier to acquire the mix of knowledge, understanding and technical skills that were required to do the job. There were four key areas of knowledge and skill: 'reading' the roof or 'top', preparing the timber appropriate to the prevailing roof conditions, 'reading' the coal to understand how it lay, and then developing the skills to be able to extract it. It took years of experience before a collier was able to do all these things competently. As one colliery manager explained:

> "Oh, you were taught. In the timbering the craft was; and working then on the face ... Now you had to be taught those things. A stranger coming in, however scientific he was, he'd have to be taught that, however intelligent he was. You were trained to understand the layering of the coal, to know where to look for it, and how to get at it when you find it."

The degree of skill required in preparing the timber needed to hold up the roof while the collier worked the coal was deceptive; for example, this part of the job involved understanding the qualities of different types of timber, and how to put it up. As one collier explained:

> "If you had a good boy he would get [done] a good part of the work that the man does. Only he can't do the technical, the timbering properly."

Another explained how trainees would be trained in timbering by their mentors:

> "Well, they would put you ... to measure a post, to cut a post, to make a [lid], to shave a piece of wood until it was flat each side so that you could put it on top of the post to hold the roof. They would teach you to notch timber which was one of the most highly specialised jobs ... they would teach you how to angle it, to put the timber up exactly where it was [to go] to do the best jobs. Oh, it was highly skilled work."

The skills required of the repairers are described by Bert Coombes, the author of two memoirs of the industry:

> ... they study the job ... walking under the broken roof to watch for cracks and gauge what stones must be barred down and which roof can be supported with timber.... Then they select timber because of its bends being suitable and its grain being the proper way. The timber must be sliced so that it will wedge tighter with pressure and stood on a slope to answer the fall of the ground. Any faulty angling would mean the supports would spring from under the pressure instead of taking it square and true. (Coombes, 1944, p 25)

Coal extraction in a non-mechanised pit also required considerable skill, as described by W.H. Taylor (one of those interviewees whose oral histories are collected in the South Wales Miners Library):

> Coal-cutting ... was a very skilled operation. You see in a coal seam there are several types of joints; there is what they call the face, which is the smooth side of it, and opposite to the face the grains going in like the grains in wood ... and they call that the ends ... the face and the ends [are] at right angles.

There was a craft to cutting coal using a pick:

> ... some days you could be fortunate ... if you had a pretty active roof and there was an amount of subsidence, the coal would crush and it would be easy to mine, and your chief worry would be the control of the roof. But other times you would have to hole it ... or undercut it. You would lie on your side and hack away and hole it under as much as a yard.

Coombes explained how difficult it was to exercise this skill in the cramped conditions in which most colliers worked:

> My mate lay on his side and cut under the coal. It took me weeks to learn the way of swinging elbows and twisting wrists without moving my shoulders. (Coombes, 1939, p 34)

The acquisition of all of these demanding competences (on which a worker's very life depended) took place in an entirely informal system: there were no apprenticeships, no classroom instruction, and no paid trainers (although the collier who provided informal training would eventually benefit from having a trained assistant – see Rees, 1996), and certainly no certification. The mentoring system proved itself to be very effective for training in non-mechanised pits where coal was extracted by hand and timber supports were used, but the informal training system proved to be incapable of coping with later changes in technology and work organisation.

Between 1913 and 1929 the proportion of coal cut by machine rose from 1% to 9%, and by 1938 it was up to 26%. Over the same period (1913-38) the number of coal cutters rose from 115 to 535 and the number of conveyors rose from 61 to 1,306 (Boyns, 1995, p 232). The new skills which were required to operate these machines could not be acquired in the informal mentoring system. Coombes became one of the first men to operate a coal-cutting machine in South Wales. His training consisted of a day helping an American engineer put together the machine which he was to operate and then:

The American gave me a booklet, explained the workings of the machine and the electric circuit, then I had a trial run.

Thereafter,

I was given a blue paper vesting authority for the handling of machinery and electricity, and found myself a coal-cutter operator.

In fact, Coombes taught himself about the machine by a process of study and trial and error:

Every hour of the day I was learning things about that machine, and in spare hours I used to study the diagrams in the booklet. I had to find out from experience and that was often painful. I learned to respect electricity – but only after I had been knocked down by it twice and had days when my wrists and ankles were made useless by the shocks. (Coombes, 1939, pp 110-11)

The colliers found that these new machines "did the very hard slogging" and "would accomplish in two

minutes ... what a collier could do by working hard all day" (Coombes, 1939, p 108) and soon the old skills and knowledge were not required. For example, the noise of the new machinery meant that it was now impossible for colliers to 'read' the roof:

The drawback was in the added danger, because we could not hear the roof cracking and ... there was the likelihood of it falling any second. (Coombes, 1939, pp 108-9)

For miners who ultimately relied "on their experience to tell them when it is time to drop everything and run" their understanding of the sounds of the roof was vital. Coombes was buried three times in a week because of the new machine (Coombes, 1944, p 15; 1939, p 120).

The oral histories of the men who witnessed the mechanisation of the South Wales pits show that while the informal training system could not cope with the change in technology no systematic effort was made to replace it with a more formal system. The effects of this breakdown were not restricted to a skills deficit. Now new recruits to the industry no longer learned a range of skills alongside an experienced collier but were simply used to shovel coal on to a conveyor. As a result, on reaching 'a man's age', the new recruit was not skilled and yet his wages were now too high for the task he was undertaking, so his labour was unwanted (Coombes, 1944, p 58). The traditional system of bringing on the next generation of colliers began to break down.

By the end of the Second World War there was a call for "a complete overhaul of the system of mining education and training in Wales" and complaints that "[t]here has never been any attempt to equip the miner with the knowledge, skill and training which is indispensable" (Roose Williams, c1945). Mining education was still the province of mangers and officials and managers while "[b]oys are sent underground and have to glean from the costly world of experience their pit sense and knowledge of safety" (Roose Williams, c1945). In a comparatively short space of time all of this was to change.

After nationalisation the wholesale bureaucratisation of training in the coal industry proceeded under a new corporatist regime (Rees, 1996). Health and Safety issues figured prominently in the new training system which also had a prominent place for apprenticeships, including, after 1960, non-craft apprenticeships. Our survey of three localities in South Wales in 1997 which provides details of 3,787 paid employment (or self-employment) episodes (full- and part-time) reveals the extent to which this pattern of formalisation was repeated in other industries. These spells are described as 'work episodes' in the analysis that follows.

According to our survey data, work-based training has not increased in frequency since 1945, remaining at just more than 39% of all work episodes which involved some sort of training. Work-based training was skewed towards jobs undertaken earlier in life (but this fact does not materially alter our conclusion that there is no evidence of an increase in work-based training).

Table 1 shows the percentage of particular age cohorts (taking age at the time of the start of the episode) receiving training in each decade (ignoring the 1940s and 1990s as outliers). The table confirms that training is less likely with greater age – for example in the 1980s 42% of 15+, 39% of 25+ and 33% of 35+ had training – but there is no clear evidence of an age-related cohort effect in the 39% of all episodes which involved some sort of training. There is a suggestion that training may be more common for the 35+ age group but then there is the problem of recency of recall.

Table 1: Training by age cohort (1950-89)

Age cohort	Total numbers	Percentage receiving training			
		1950s	1960s	1970s	1980s
15-24	2,204	40	45	49	42
25-34	874	39	30	33	39
35-44	505	–	27	22	33

Of all work episodes, 22% received Health and Safety training, and this proportion has grown consistently from 15% in the 1940s to 28% in the 1990s (see Table 2). This increase makes Health and Safety training unlike all other categories of work-based training. For example, there has been no increase in short in-service courses such as those now common in information technology training. In-service training (half-day and IT courses) has remained remarkably stable at somewhere near 23% and nor has induction training increased, remaining at 18% of work episodes. Training considered useful to another employer (in that it would enhance careership/employability) has actually decreased marginally over time and now accounts for 7% of episodes. The proportion of work episodes having any other type of training (apart from Health and Safety and in-service) is 24% and has been relatively constant over time, but peaking in the 1960s. Around 16% had training to do the job better and this proportion is also constant over time.

Table 2: Trends in training type (1940-96) (%)

	1940s	1950s	1960s	1970s	1980s	1990s
Health and Safety training	15	17	20	22	23	28
Other training	24	25	27	26	21	24
Any training	34	40	41	41	37	40

Work-based training occurs more often in lengthy spells of employment and this is especially true of both more prolonged training and transferable training. On average, people do not receive training that enhances their employability after the age of 22. When the length of employment is taken into account (by dividing the number of formal training episodes by the number of months employed), there is still no change in the proportion of substantive training over time. There is a small but significant negative correlation between age and frequency of training (–7%).

There has been a relative decline in the frequency of any type of training episode lasting five or more days from 18% in the 1950s to 11% in the 1980s (see Table 3). This agrees with the report of the DfEE (1995) which shows how the frequency of job-related training has increased from 1980 to 1994 for example, but this growth has been mainly in courses off-the-job on employers' premises lasting less than a week (Gorard et al, 1997b).

Table 3: Training lasting five days or longer (1940-96) (%)

	1940s	1950s	1960s	1970s	1980s	1990s
5+ days training	17	18	18	17	11	12

Of the longer episodes, there is still no increase in attempted certification (see Table 4).

Table 4: Participants in longer training episodes attempting qualifications (%)

	1940s	1950s	1960s	1970s	1980s	1990s
Attempted qualifications	60	51	52	49	55	54

When this is examined as a proportion of all work episodes it is clear that certification has *declined* along with substantive training. As the 'raw' frequency of training episodes increases, their relative length and certification decreases (see Table 5).

Table 5: Participants in all training episodes attempting qualifications (%)

	1940s	1950s	1960s	1970s	1980s	1990s
Attempted qualifications	10	9	9	8	6	6

The vast majority of these longer training spells are paid for by the employer, but there is some indication that this proportion is in decline, and is being replaced by government training schemes (see Table 6). In the 1940s, 94% of episodes were employer-funded (or the employee could not recall when asked in our survey). The peak was in the 1970s with 96%, and the lowest was in the 1990s with 88%. Finally, 92% of these spells were in working hours and there was no change over time, and 66% of spells were provided by the employer (as opposed to private firm, further education, government scheme, etc), and there was no change over time.

Table 6: Participation in government training (%)

	1940s	1950s	1960s	1970s	1980s	1990s
Government training courses	0	5	3	2	5	11

To sum up the survey results on formal, work-based training, Health and Safety training is increasing and such short employer-based courses are typical of the growth over time. New training is brief, prescribed by law, non-transferable, and non-certified (at least not according to our respondents' interpretation of this term). The costs of training have shifted from employers towards government agencies (and schools and colleges). However, it would be dangerous to conclude from this that we have laid bare changing patterns of training provision within individual firms. Both the industrial structure and the gender division of labour within South Wales have changed radically during the period concerned. The decline of employment in those sectors where formal training, and especially apprenticeship training, had become general was accompanied by an increase in employment in sectors with very different training regimes and large numbers of women employees (Rees, 1993). Given these caveats (and others, for example, the increased availability of training and education outside work episodes) it is no surprise that, at the level of the individual employer, and even throughout some industrial sectors, there has clearly been an increase in the formalisation of training.

Many of the training officers we interviewed recalled that formal training in the past consisted only of apprentice training and some management courses. Nevertheless, by the end of this period, there was a growing recognition of both the needs and benefits of more formalised training which was informed by the increasing centralisation of organisations and by changing work practices. Growing exposure to foreign competition revealed deficiencies in both operating procedures and production processes and sensitised management to the possibilities of training, and foreign competitors (including those investing in South Wales) were perceived to have superior training regimes. However, in the 1980s the new emphasis on training was not sufficiently established to be able to resist the effects of restructuring brought on by recession.

Some embryonic training regimes were under threat from restructuring and cost-cutting exercises and where there was a continued commitment to training, this tended to be in foreign-owned companies, particularly those associated with the automotive industry.

Nevertheless, the formalisation of training in the 1990s was clearly apparent in the work histories of respondents included in the subsample chosen for re-interview. One man aged 38 had worked in the steel industry for 15 years without any formal training after initial training on entry, but during the last six years his employer brought in numerous training programmes. A nurse recalled the dearth of (post-qualifying) training early in her career: in those days there was no need for constant up-dating or specialisation, whereas now there is a continuous need to update one's knowledge of new procedures (for example, in her role as a practice nurse). In these two examples (as in the archive and key informant data) increased formality has accompanied a perceived change in job characteristics (ie changing technology and/or work organisation).

Informants from the training sector also claimed that the old pattern of informal learning by watching is increasingly inappropriate to the modern manufacturing environment; for example, changes in technology and manufacturing processes mean that workers have to be able to work to very detailed, written job specifications. However, there are other factors at work in increasing formality, for example the 1974 Health and Safety at Work Act. A woman aged 37 talks about how, in the years before this legislation, she was "shown what to do and then got on with it" and how she and her colleagues were "left to our own devices", where "if you chopped a couple of fingers off, you chopped a couple of fingers off". Another woman aged 49 describes how learning by experience in a dangerous work environment involved somebody losing a finger. Similarly, a man aged 64 describes his training as common sense "because no one was shown anything" and this involved him "losing a finger on the back of the shears".

Interview and key informant data provide examples from the 1990s of employers disregarding any knowledge or competences brought to a job by

new recruits and trusting only in their own training (particularly at induction) to turn out identically-equipped workers (examples include foreign-owned manufacturers and national chain organisations such as supermarkets). There are also examples of occupations where in-service training seems to have become an end in itself. The training coordinator of one supermarket reported that, at the national level, the company felt that one of the major reasons why it lost its leading market position was that rivals had better in-store training. Lack of emphasis on training reflected complacency about its position as number one retailer and training was now seen as a major element in the drive to regain its former position, but the staff are not necessarily ready for the culture change:

> "A lot of people who come into [the store] say, 'Look I only came here to stack shelves, I don't want to do workbooks and things, I don't want to go back to school' ... so it's very difficult ... we've got workbooks for just about everything, a tremendous amount of them, I'm afraid. Some people just do not want to do this, it's very difficult then to encourage them and again that is part of my job. I am enthusiastic about my job and again I think that does tend to wear off on people."

The subsample who were re-interviewed in depth reveal respondents' experience of *informal* training.

It should be recalled from the survey findings that most new jobs involved no training of any type, not even a half day of Health and Safety training. Perhaps the most common response to questions about training for new tasks was that such new tasks were picked up through 'common sense'. This response came from individuals in a wide variety of situations, from a barrister in pupilage, to pharmacists on drug counters, to lathe operators, school teachers, sales representatives and care assistants. One woman became a clerk, then an assistant to a dog-breeder, and then a small-holding farmer without any formal training at any stage. Another respondent who reported no formal training was trusted with the accounts of a medium-sized firm, and later set up her own playgroup for children. Another respondent was a cook in the Army, using only her knowledge from cooking at home for the family. Although a few complained of being "thrown in at the deep end" and not having "a clue what I was doing", the conclusions that most of these respondents drew from their experiences was that, in their view, formal training was unnecessary and that experience was everything. However, many respondents did describe more formal induction, and, although it is difficult to judge, there are some indications that the survey may have underestimated the amount of such training.

One, a woman in her 50s who left school at 15 with her parents' blessing and had no lifetime qualifications, had this to say of her jobs in haberdashery:

"Once you learnt how to do things, it was more or less all the same.... What you done, you done your training for a month of how to sew and this, that and the other and used heavy machines. That was it. You didn't get no more training again.... I mean the thing is I can go right through from a complete suite from the arms, backs, outside backs, cushions, front borders, seats; so I mean, you know, through the years I mean, you know, you pick it up."

A man in his 60s left school at 14 chiefly for economic reasons, like so many others. He also had no qualifications, but had a very successful career in British Steel Tinplate, being promoted several times and moving between areas of work despite receiving no formal training:

"You learn as you get along.... You got to train yourself and you use your hands and ears. No one came along and said, 'you mustn't do this' or 'you mustn't do that'.... I mean common sense will tell you not to do certain things.... I can pick up most things purely by watching someone else doing it.... I did my own wiring in my house [a smart house on the edge of the Brecon Beacons]."

Another man was a coal-cutter who had to give up when his local mine suffered a catastrophe:

"There was an explosion in Six Bells – can you remember it? And there was quite a few dead. Well, we was actually working, they were working towards us from Six Bells ... and we was only a matter of from here to that wall away from them when it happened. So I thought that was enough so then, um, I came out and went to be a manager with Premier Cheques. Used to have a cheque and they could go into the shop and buy clothes. Premier Cheques it was called at that time and I was manager in Tredegar, and they moved me over to Brynmawr."

The importance of this story is that this man received no training at all in order to change career (apparently successfully) from being a coal-miner to service sector manager. He told us that he could have had five or six jobs, and there are many such examples from an era of full employment of what would now seem extraordinary career changes involving no retraining.

A signalman on the railways in the 1950s became a station master with a staff of six "doing everything – income tax, bills, pay, everything", and learnt his tasks "just by spending a fortnight with the chap who was doing it before me ... and I'd issue all tickets". This made it difficult for him to deal with the unexpected:

"Somebody once, I wonder if it was a put-up-job, brought me a bike to send to Ireland and I ended up sending it to Dudley, the next station down the line, because I couldn't deal with it."

An assistant in a pharmacy found the job very difficult to start with and reported no subsequent training:

"It was about three or four months before I could really get into and know ... and knew what I was doing, but as I say I'm giving out drugs now that you don't know really what they're for and they're given different brand names. And you're not really given the generic name of the drug so there's no ... unless you ask which ... we're a very, very busy pharmacy anyway and there's not really a lot of time for training."

Another woman with several job changes has had no training, despite being aged 34. She first worked as a typist in the car industry, and learned as she 'went along', and then moved to work as a clerk to an insurance firm:

"Well they gave me a manual to work the computer. I just learned myself. But I managed.... I had a manual to work it all out. And I wasn't computer-minded so I was right in at the deep end."

She moved to become a branch administrator for a national sports company, a move which involved additional duties, such as being expected to take up responsibility straightaway for installing a new networked computer system, again with no training:

"And, um, I had to teach the branch members how to use the computer and also my manager because he didn't really take an interest at all."

She describes this job as 'dead-end' and hopes to apply for a post in the wages department in a new electronics factory in Port Talbot.

Even where vocational training is apparently available, it can be in name only. Like many other respondents, a young woman made this complaint of Youth Training (and it is clear from her later description of 'marvellous' training courses that she is able to be discriminating in her criticisms):

"It was a complete waste of time. They didn't teach you to do anything. You had to learn it for yourself. They didn't show you what to do. It was a case of 'here's the stuff – have a go'.... There's supervisors walking around and foremen but all they were there for was drinking coffee and having a fag. They were a complete waste of time. [My mates] all thought the same."

Sometimes people took a job with a promise of training which was not kept. One woman who started work at a florist's shop had been assured that she would receive training by her employer:

"She was going to, and she promised me faithfully and they promised me this, that and the other, and when it eventually materialised like I said 'what about me signing on at the Tech?' She said, 'oh sorry, no, we can't afford to let you have the time off'. I was working 8.30 am to 5.30 pm six days a week."

In other cases, training was available for some, but not others. A woman from Bridgend described the pattern when working in her local hospital:

"No. You had a funny situation there. If you went in as a clerk with five O levels then you could do further training, but if you were a shorthand typist [like her], you tended to stay."

A 30-year-old woman who started her career as a postgraduate student received no research training in return for her fees. She was also given

responsibility for undergraduate teaching with no supervision and no training:

"I suppose I recognised what I thought was good in tutors and one in particular I thought had been very successful in the way that he taught, and I tried to put together what I thought was good and rule out what was bad. All of us who were graduates spent ages sitting around talking about what constitutes good teaching and a good tutorial."

When she took up a lectureship at a Welsh university, she received only Health and Safety training in the form of fire drills. An 'induction day' was available, but:

"My colleagues made a big fuss – 'Why do you want to go on an induction day? It's completely useless' – and actually made it quite hard for me to go."

Eventually she was given training in how to lecture, but she had two complaints about this training. Firstly, it was too late as she had already been teaching for six years. If the training had been of any value, then it would have helped six previous cohorts of her students. Secondly, the training was aimed at those who were completely new to teaching, but was attended by experienced tutors as a precondition of getting a permanent job – perhaps the archetypal 'unnecessary learning'.

Several respondents would agree with the woman who was asked about Health and Safety training in the 1950s and 1960s: "[n]obody worried about things like that then. It's quite a new thing I think, isn't it?" Since several accounts (see above) tell of industrial injuries the growth of such training (also described above) may have been more necessary than the formalisation of other types. One woman who was moved to work on the police switchboard was given no training – "nothing at all" – but the switchboard was so old that "it would give you electric shocks and cut out".

Not all respondents were happy that they received no training. Although most appear to feel that training was not necessary, even for quite responsible roles, some would have welcomed the formal reassurance:

Interviewer: *"And you were just working by yourself, no supervisor or...?"*

"No."

Interviewer: *"Nothing at all?"*

"No."

Interviewer: *"So you were ... you went straight from college straight into that job and you just had to find your feet. Was it, I mean...?"*

"That's right.... I found it difficult and I used to worry about it, so I was glad when I got another job and left there."

On the other hand, when the 38-year-old steelworker (discussed above) who had received all sorts of training in the steel industry in the last few years, was asked if he felt as though he was 'multi-skilled' he explained how he was "jack of all trades and master of none". The nurse (discussed above) explained the increased amount in-service training in the NHS as a result of the new need for constant updating or specialisation, but was disparaging about initial, certificated nursing training. She felt the training she had had was directly relevant to the job and made better nurses than the sort of training people now received which excluded important elements and meant that new nurses did not know how to do their jobs – and had to learn on the job by copying the old hands.

Like others, including the barrister, this secondary school teacher apparently found such informal training more valuable than its formal variant:

"I think it is a case of ... it is a case of watching other people. I think I probably learnt more from watching others since I'm out of college than I ever did when I was in college. And also I think I've moulded my teaching now and even then on the teachers that I was taught by. The teachers that I ... sort of my older years at school you know when I was perhaps 14, 15, 16; some of those I can remember I either liked their teaching method or I didn't and I adapted that."

It is a reasonable inference from the interviews and the archival data that several of our respondents would subscribe to some degree to the opinion that

informal learning may in fact be necessary learning while this is not always the case with formal training. In part they wondered whether formalisation reflected the internal imperative of the 'audit society' (Power, 1997) rather than substantive rationality. This concern was also evident in interviews with key informants, especially when they were discussing NVQs.

NVQs of course represent not only the certification of informal learning but the formal recognition of the pattern (once general in coal-mining – see above) of workers passing on skills to other workers. A training manager in manufacturing thought NVQs to be a positive development since there should be recognition of informal learning on the job (as an educational achievement) but in practice the employees showed a huge span of abilities and employee responses had been very mixed. The principal of a further education college thought there were perhaps 6,000 qualifications in the NVQ, many of which have only been awarded once or never, making NVQ a qualification which was too specific to regional and particular workplace conditions. Another key informant gave the example of a story in the press illustrated with a picture of 40 employees all proudly brandishing their new qualifications when in fact only one of the 40 knew they had the NVQ when they were called to the boardroom and given the certificate.

Further evidence of the imperatives of the 'audit society' might be found among the respondents who told us they could do their jobs without training and those who were having to certify their skills to maintain their jobs. A 16-year-old male respondent's knowledge of gardening and mechanics, derived from his hobbies and training given by family members, gave him the skills he needed for his job in landscape gardening. When the interviewer suggested that he get his skills certified, the respondent reported that, as a result of a bad experience with careers advice and an early mismatched placement, he did not want anything to do with the formal system. A 20-year-old male respondent was asked to conduct a survey for his local bus company and missed the training session. His job went smoothly and was performed without the need for the initial training. A 22-year-old man works as plasterer, bricklayer and window framer, all of which skills he has learned from his boss through a sort of informal apprenticeship. He has been advised to get these skills certified by his employer in case the company folds and he needs another employer to recognise his skills. A 24-year-old electrician is becoming qualified for an occupation that he is already successfully following. He lacks the written or theoretical skills. A 35-year-old man works as a voluntary care assistant but is having to gain the qualifications to certify to others he can do the job he is already performing (this will be a difficult process because he has difficulty reading and writing).

Informal learning outside the workplace

The archive material (selected from Burge et al, 1998) shows that not all the informal learning in the workplace took the form of vocational training. The teaching and learning that went on in the pit was far broader than that necessary for mining coal or safety. The relationship of trust that developed was an essential part of extending the informal process of teaching and learning of mining practice to influence a broader range of social values and attitudes (see Chapter 3 in this volume by Stephen Baron and colleagues which also makes this point).

On his first pay-day Jim Vale received a sovereign from John Davies. As he paid him Davies said:

> *"Do you see that shed over there? ... That belongs ... to the Federation. The Miners belong to that ... and that's where they pay their dues.... Go over ... and make yourself a member of an organisation."*

In this learning milieu there were close associations between coal-mining and union membership and between learning to read the roof and recognising the benefits of education. Wil Jon Edwards described the importance of the 'double parting', the area of the colliery where miners took their breaks. It was the centre for gossip, jokes and serious discussion:

> *"It was at the double parting that I first heard the names of Herbert Spencer and Charles Darwin.... There were occasions at the double parting when religion, science and the rest were put in cold storage, being ousted by political events."*

Here young men could witness (although they were not allowed to contribute to) discussions between their older colleagues which might turn to analyses of the respective merits of the poets Meredith and Kipling.

In the years before 1914 it was that minority of coal-miners who considered themselves 'advanced men' who applied a class analysis towards education, including technical education. They were not interested in the opportunities for learning which were geared to individual self-advancement within the coal industry through the acquisition of technical qualifications (cf Chapter 4 in this volume). They were interested in addressing much more fundamental questions about the colliery in which they worked, the company which owned it, the economics of the industry and the workings of capitalism. Such interests might lead them to see technical education in a very different, and negative, light. In 1907 a small group of South Wales miners studying at Ruskin College opposed the idea that the South Wales Miners Federation, the miners' trade union, should contribute towards a new School of Mines at Pontypridd. Five years later A.J. Cook addressed the Pontypridd Trades and Labour Council on whether education was in the interests of 'the boss or the worker' (Lewis, 1993, p 60; Davies, 1987, p 18).

After the Great War the interests of the 'advanced men' were more widely embraced by miners across the coalfield. When Harold Watkins was appointed in 1920 as a tutor in economics and allied studies by Glamorgan Education Committee, he found that his students told him that their war experiences had "forced them to do some hard thinking and made them determined 'to find out about things'". While they might once have been motivated to study commercial subjects or mine management, their interests now lay in other directions and Watkins detected a "tense earnestness" in his evening class students and their increasingly urgent desire to get to grips with economics. Those miners' leaders who felt that technical education served the needs of business, and that the needs of business and workers were inimical, now articulated their views clearly. Almost from its inception in 1923 the *Colliery Workers' Magazine,* the new journal of the South Wales Miners' Federation, included articles which were critical of technical education which was said to be serving the interests of "the quick-witted magnate" for whom "[t]o subscribe to technical institutions is money well spent"(Ted Williams, *Colliery Workers' Magazine*, 1923, p 191). The author of this broadsheet returned to the theme a year later when, referring to technical education, he declared that "objection is taken to any scheme which purports to increase production in order that capitalism may continue to further exploit wage labour" (Ted Williams, *Colliery Workers' Magazine*, 1924, p 205).

According to our survey, which covers the period 1945-96, a self-directed interest in history or politics purely as a hobby had disappeared entirely by the 1990s. Our data suggests that the people Eraut describes as being particularly adept at acquiring necessary knowledge and competences through informal learning within the workplace are also good at learning (and applying this knowledge) outside the workplace (1997; also see Eraut et al, 1998a, 1998b).

The data reveals that the average age for starting an informal (non-participatory, non-certified) episode of learning (eg 'hobby') is 29; 19% of people reported at least one such episode, and there appears to be no change in frequency of these episodes over time although there are substantial changes over time in the proportion reporting sustained leisure study or practice. The figures are unreliable but there are indications that 'hobbies' as such are declining in frequency, although pursuits in the categories of sports, animals, electronic and computing interests have grown (from 20% to 60% of the total between them); voluntary work, officials of local societies, council activity have remained constant (at around 7%), as has haberdashery, sewing and so on (11%). The clear declines have been in gardening (18% to 0), art and photography (15% to 0), and history or politics (8% to 0). These figures relate to the decade in which the interest started and many of those who became interested in gardening or photography in the 1950s are still pursuing this hobby.

Around 50% of all respondents took a qualification at the end of compulsory schooling, but 55% of those with leisure interests did so too. The difference is small but significant. However, those with interests (hobbyists) had exactly the same

frequency of continuing their full-time education past the school-leaving age. In statistical terms, formal education is replacing hobbies, and self-directed study has reduced, while staying-on rates at school have increased. This interpretation is backed up by all other available indications. Of those who continue to further education, hobbyists are *less* likely to take a qualification. They get fewer substantive training episodes in their first two jobs, and, even allowing for this, they are less likely to take a qualification when training for their first two jobs. They are much more likely to take a non-continuous episode of education or training which is not work-related, but less likely to take a qualification as a result.

Further interview data illustrates how valuable informal learning outside the workplace might be in terms of knowledge and skills which are nevertheless relevant to employment. One man, for whom there was little separation between work and home, had taught himself pottery (with his wife), electrolysis for metallising, simple electronics, wax casting, and furniture modelling. He had a perspex-cutting room in his house, a silver-plated frog in his living room, and once made a scale model of the Challenger space shuttle which is now on the desk of a four star general in NASA. In some cases he had been successfully employed on the basis of self-taught skills:

"So as I say ... I haven't got a GCE or a BSc or whatever they're called these days ... but as I say you don't have to be academic to be able to do things.... Because of the books I read and I like reading science books et cetera, and with the television my favourite channel is the Discovery Channel."

"It's the same with the French polishing, you see. I used to do it as a favour. I got a book from the library. I had a blind chappie who was a pianist, like, and he used to tune pianos and doing them up. He asked me if I knew anything about polishing and I said 'not the foggiest'. So I went to the library, got a book on it, we got the French polish and promptly went into business. It was just a sideline when I was working for the printers."

This story of a genuinely multi-skilled but mainly self-taught interviewee is very similar to that reported in Gorard et al (1997c), where a self-taught plasterer and electrician, who loved opera but worked as a steel foundryman, explained how he had read about the care of the 7,000 bedding plants he had in his garden:

"Well, you see when I was doing those I used to send off for those books. Once a month you get books from them. They come in volumes. There are 12 volumes. So if ever I was stuck I look, I used to look through the books and say 'Oh', read it up, 'oh that's the way to do it'. It's the same with the bricklaying. I ordered a bricklaying book and I read it up ... with plastering now a friend of mine is in the library and she got me a book, so ... if I got to do a job I'm not quite sure I get the book and read it up and say 'oh well' this is the way."

"Like that wall was all different when I'd done it the first time. Then we went to Porthcawl one day and we see these walls and she [his wife] said 'yeah it's nice – could you do that on the wall?' She said, 'well there's a lot of cracks there'. So we took the old wall off and I plastered it across, removed all the fittings, fitted them all in and plastered it all off and it's been there since. She likes it but then I had to do the room in there then.... Just put a couple of mouldings on the wall."

"I like doing things. I think if you like doing something it's no hardship then. You know, time flies."

Another man told us:

"I like to build these little things. I've got something going on here look. This is a low-powered – that's not part of it – but this is a low-powered transmitter-receiver. That's the sort of thing I like doing, but that's part of a project I got out of a magazine."

This 62-year-old man taught himself "radio technology – a lifelong hobby" – and took night courses in maths when he was working; he has learned Morse code and radio construction, and, after borrowing a book on calculus and algebra from his library, wants to start an Open University maths course. His hobbies in maths and then radios stem from early childhood interests and, he told us, as a reaction against his maths teacher telling him he couldn't join the maths club. A 24-year-old man's leisure interests include drama (which he would love to be involved in professionally); producing publicity for a string quartet (advertising and a website for appearances at weddings); self-taught computing, DIY and car maintenance.

Although the differences can be overemphasised, there is a pattern in these stories in the types of skills and activities undertaken by men and women. To some extent the gendered differences in the distribution of learning trajectories (see Gorard et al, 1998c) may be replicated by gendered differences in informal learning outside work. A woman in her 40s reported taking a course in German which was uncertificated, which was how she preferred it since she was studying primarily for interest and "tourism" and had "never taken to languages at school". This took up three hours of one evening in the week. She also sews and reads a lot at home. In addition:

"I'm very involved in my local church with the Mothers' Union and Young Wives' Group and ... I'm at the moment treasurer of the Mothers' Union.... I've been treasurer twice of the Wives' Group and secretary. I've also been secretary of the Fête committee, and as I say I was secretary of the PTA ... I'm on the social committee to do with the church, so that takes up a lot of my time."

Another woman of a similar age has taught herself to crochet and do quilting from books, building on skills in knitting and sewing she gained as a child. She organises a local ladies club and a coffee club to raise funds for her children's school. Again there are similarities with her earlier work as a bookkeeper which she undertook with no reported training, and where she taught herself how National Insurance worked from pamphlets, but she speaks for several respondents when she alludes to the pressures on her time:

"Yes, I think when you've got a family you tend not to.... Can't seem to get around to do all the things I would like to do."

A similar story emerged in an interview with a woman in her 50s who started explaining how she taught herself to play the organ:

"When we came here ... there were two organists and neither could play at this funeral for some reason. He said you've got to play. Fortunately there was a week in between and every day I went down, this was a very old pipe organ. I went home in tears and said 'I can't play it, it's a completely different ball game to playing the piano. You wouldn't believe it ... middle C isn't middle C and

when you take your finger off it stops. I just can't'. But I did it."

She runs a sewing class for the Mothers' Union, does all the brassing for the local church and launders their linen. She is Brown Owl of the local Brownie pack, and governor of her local infant school. She reports no special training to take on any of these roles, which she describes as "just inheriting".

One woman who runs groups of Brownies, Rainbows and Guides described the skills she has developed as a result:

"Patience – patience and the understanding of children. How their minds start to work, to be honest, because I know you've got children of your own but none of these children are the same…. And managing groups of kiddies is a difficult skill isn't it?"

Yet another interviewee took over the aerobics class she was attending, and is now employed as a tutor in Ogwr. The pay was so good that she gave up her job as a cashier to travel the borough providing classes. Again, she has no special training and mentioned no earlier qualifications but now, at the age of 53, she has gained an A grade in GCSE French, and is studying for A level, aiming for a higher qualification:

"Then my dream is … Brian and I, we're going to – when the boys don't need us any more – we're going to get a job on a camp site in France. He's going to leave Fords. He's going to be the handyman and the person that does the garden, and I'm going to be the receptionist and I'm going to talk French to everybody."

In some cases, people's ambitions are more prosaic. One woman who was illiterate when she left school and throughout her first marriage, simply wanted to learn to read:

"Mine started to get better really when I was having my first son. I was in hospital for nigh on six months and I mean hospital is quite boring. I started to read. I read a lot now but I find I like to go over the books a couple of times because I'm always picking up things that I've missed before."

A woman in a similar position was taught to read by her husband, and can now read a tabloid newspaper, a skill which she was keen to demonstrate, while a woman in her 60s described how she had always been a 'reader', and she reads all day, every day (anything accept a 'cowboy' book). She has no formal post-compulsory education or training, and, needless to, say no qualifications.

In future publications we will consider what the interview and archive data can tell us about the motivations of these men and women. For example, the barrister in pupilage taught himself because he felt he could make quicker progress in this way than on courses where he had to wait for others. Similarly, a 29-year-old man who is a local councillor and school governor taught himself how to use a computer (for work), because he didn't want to take a class in it and wait for others. In future we can use our interview data to complement the archive material and investigate the effect of families and communities (all sorts of communities, not simply occupational ones) on learning identities.

On the basis of future work we may well conclude that the individuals who *make a career* of informal learning do it because learning is part of their wider identities (wider than work, that is): they learn at work because they like to learn everywhere, and what they learn is the necessary knowledge and skills they need to achieve something, whether this be a practical achievement or self-transformation.

Conclusions

As Eraut's chapter in this volume indicates, valuable learning, including learning for work, happens when people are not being schooled or formally trained. The skills and knowledge that were passed on by the informal mentoring system in the South Wales coalfield before mechanisation could not have been passed on in a formal way. Without these skills new recruits could not cut coal, or even ensure their own safety, yet the informal system that passed these skills on had to satisfy demands that were far more advanced than those made in most of the jobs in light manufacturing and the service sector, which replaced traditional industries like coal-mining. Our archival data on the mechanisation of the mines, and survey data on the postwar boom years, shows how people learned to do complicated new things without any formal training system. The individuals involved may not always have liked the experience (although they may sometimes be judging it with hindsight informed by more modern expectations of formal training), and may sometimes have found it painful and even dangerous, but they *did* learn.

The introduction of a bureaucratised training system in coal-mining followed the nationalisation of the industry. Many thought this long overdue, and the process was not confined to coal-mining, but it did not signal the beginning of a generalised movement to train more and more workers for longer periods of time. There was more Health and Safety training (mainly as a result of legislation) but there was no overall increase in training. This was in part due to the subsequent decline of employment in industries such as coal-mining that had introduced apprenticeships. The loss of training here counter-balanced the increase in training in sectors where employment was expanding. In any event, where training increased this was unlikely to be because employers had been converted to the necessity of introducing training in their existing jobs. It took many decades of complaints about the need for training to lead to such a process in the coal mines and there has, as yet, been no comparable process elsewhere in British industry. The main stimulus to formal training in the second half of the 20th century has been the generation of new jobs which are deemed to require training from their inception.

This process may well involve a very different logic – perhaps closely related to the idea of 'lifelong learning as social control' discussed by Coffield (1999) – to the one that demands that training be introduced into jobs which are already in existence in order to make workers more productive. Some concerns about the importance of training had been expressed over the years in our study areas but our research produced little evidence of this sort of commitment to training outside the plants established by foreign direct investment. The alternative logic for training (which sees it as a necessary adjunct of recruitment to the types of jobs being created in the private service sector, for example) typically produces formal, short courses which have a very specific focus and are not capable of creating transferable skills or even of making people more productive.

It is sometimes claimed that the type of training philosophy that is reflected in such developments is much more interested in inculcating norms and values than in passing on knowledge and skills. However, the comparative historical method used here raises doubts about the value of such training as occupational socialisation. Consider the way, before mechanisation, that the informal mentoring system was able to ensure the succession of each new generation of miners. This was replaced by apprenticeship and a formal internal labour market which had a similar effect but this too entered into rapid decline in time. By comparison with these historical systems, new, very short and closely-focused forms of training seem woefully inadequate. They may be predicated on the importance of inculcating workplace culture, and the priority of socialisation into a particular organisation, but suffer by comparison with the socialisation practices they effectively replace.

It comes as no surprise that large numbers of our respondents continue to report that they teach themselves how to do their jobs. Their experiences are neatly encapsulated in the familiar tale of being trained long after they have learned how to do the job in question, even being trained simply in order to get the paper credential which has suddenly become necessary to 'prove' that they can do the job. This reinforces our observation that necessary learning in work is often something that individuals arrange for themselves without help from their employers. It also supports our suggestion that much formal training may be unnecessary. It is clear that formal training – for example, the National Coal Board's (NCB's) apprenticeship system – can provide opportunities for necessary learning but it is not at all clear that the short, non-transferable training now on offer is capable of providing such opportunities.

Rich and effective learning – learning that involves socialisation, for example – spills over into the lives people lead outside work. The archival data documented the coal-miners' realisation, around the time of the First World War, that education might be seen as a mechanism for increasing the rate of exploitation and even for maintaining wider capitalist social relations. Again this brings to mind the argument which has reappeared in the course of *The Learning Society Programme* and which is articulated in the idea of 'lifelong learning as social control' (Coffield, 1999). Our data shows that at one time ideas such as these had currency in the wider population. Whereas we can now point to overwhelming evidence of increased formal education, there may well be much less of the broad workplace-based learning which had a large informal component and which knew no boundaries and produced lifelong learners. Some lifelong learners remain and we concluded our discussion above with some examples of these men and women. The recurrent point in all of their stories was that their learning had nothing to do with acquiring qualifications – this is, after all, the *sine qua non* of informal learning – and everything to do with acquiring necessary knowledge and skills.

To return to the points raised in the introduction to this chapter, Eraut considers that a huge amount of learning that goes on in work is virtually unnoticed by researchers and even by employers. This learning is vitally necessary to the organisations people work for (and perhaps also to the fulfilment of the individuals concerned) but it is not acquired in any formal manner. Eraut's approach is ahistorical and does not take into account the way in which the degree of importance attached to informal learning as opposed to formal learning has changed. If increased formalisation had occurred because it is more effective in transmitting necessary knowledge and competences Eraut's thesis would be weakened. Thus far, our research does not suggest that there has been a net increase in formality while it would seem that the need for necessary learning in informal settings remains.

Much valuable and non-trivial learning already goes on, and has always gone on, outside formal programmes of instruction. This is true both at work and at leisure. If such informal learning continues to be ignored by proponents of a learning society, as it has been by the authors of the recent Green Papers (Welsh Office, 1998; DfEE, 1998) for example, then the result will be an unnecessary exclusiveness in definitions of a learning society, and an unjustifiable reliance on certification. Leisure

learning is a clear characteristic of lifelong and delayed learners (Gorard et al, 1998a), thus associated with later learning, not transitional learning (Gorard et al, 1998b). If informal learning is a characteristic of later life learners, surely it is a characteristic that creators of a learning society should seek to enhance? However, this self-reliance may be negated by the ambitions of the 'audit society'. The hobbyists are informal learners, learning at home in their spare time, not seeking certification, and not linking learning to their work, and they may be disappearing in association with the growth in formal participation. In this we agree with Pat Davies (see her chapter in this volume, and cf NIACE, 1994) that the increased certification of adult education (tied to local education authority funding criteria) may actually serve to alienate informal learners.

References

Boyns, T. (1995) 'Jigging and shaking: technical choice in the South Wales coal industry between the wars', *Welsh History Review*, vol 17, 1994-95, p 232.

Burge, A., Trottman, C. and Francis, H. (1998) *In a class of their own: Adult learning and the South Wales mining community 1900-1939*, mimeo, Swansea: University of Wales, forthcoming as: *Patterns of participation in adult education and training*, Working Paper No 14, Cardiff: School of Education, Cardiff University.

Coffield, F. (1997) 'Nine learning fallacies and their replacement by a natural strategy for lifelong learning', in F. Coffield (ed) *A national strategy for lifelong learning*, Newcastle: Department of Education, University of Newcastle, pp 3-35.

Coffield, F. (1999) *Breaking the consensus: Lifelong learning as social control*, Newcastle: Department of Education, University of Newcastle.

Coombes, B.L. (1939) *These poor hands*, London: Gollancz.

Coombes, B.L. (1944) *These clouded hills*, London: Cobbett.

Davies, P. (1987) *A. J. Cook*, Manchester: Manchester University Press.

DfEE (Department for Education and Employment) (1995) *Training statistics 1995*, London: HMSO.

DfEE (1998) *The Learning Age*, London: The Stationery Office.

Eraut, M. (1997) 'Perspectives on defining "the Learning Society"', *Journal of Education Policy*, vol 12, no 6, pp 551-8.

Eraut, M., Alderton, J., Cole, G. and Senker, P. (1998a) *Development of knowledge and skills in employment*, Research Report No 5, Brighton: Institute of Education, University of Sussex.

Eraut, M., Alderton, J., Cole, G. and Senker, P. (1998b) 'Learning from other people at work', in F. Coffield (ed) *Learning at work*, Bristol: The Policy Press.

Fevre, R., Rees, G. and Gorard, S. (1999) 'Some sociological alternatives to human capital theory and their implications for research on post-compulsory education and training', *Journal of Education and Work*, vol 12, no 2, pp 117-40.

Gallie, D. (1988) 'Introduction', in D. Gallie (ed) *Employment in Britain*, Oxford: Basil Blackwell, pp 1-10.

Girod, R. (1990) *Problems of sociology in education*, Paris: Unesco.

Gorard, S., Furlong, J., Rees, G. and Fevre, R. (1997b) *The learning society*, Working Paper No 5, Patterns of Participation in Adult Education and Training, Cardiff: School of Education, Cardiff University.

Gorard, S., Rees, G., Furlong, J. and Fevre, R. (1997a) *Outline methodology of the study*, Working Paper No 2, Patterns of Participation in Adult Education and Training, Cardiff: School of Education, Cardiff University.

Gorard, S., Rees, G., Fevre, R. and Furlong J. (1997c) *Learning trajectories: Some voices of those in transit*, Working Paper No 11, Patterns of Participation in Adult Education and Training, Cardiff: School of Education, Cardiff University.

Gorard, S., Renold, E., Rees, G., Fevre, R. and Furlong. J. (1998c) 'A gendered appraisal of the transition to a learning society in Britain', in R. Benn (ed) *Research, teaching and learning: Making corrections in the education of adults*, Leeds: Standing Conference on University Teaching and Research in the Education of Adults.

Gorard, S., Rees, G., Fevre, R. and Furlong, J. (1998a) 'Learning trajectories: travelling towards a learning society?', *International Journal of Lifelong Education*, vol 17, no 6, pp 400-10.

Gorard S., Rees G., Fevre R. and Furlong J. (1998b) 'The two components of a new learning society', *Journal of Vocational Education and Training*, vol 50, no 1, pp 5-19.

Lewis, R., (1993) *Leaders and teachers: Adult education and the challenge of labour in South Wales, 1906-1940*, Cardiff: University of Wales Press.

NIACE (National Institute of Adult Continuing Education) (1994) *Widening participation: Routes to a learning society*, NIACE Policy Discussion Paper, Leicester University.

Power, M. (1997) *The audit society*, Oxford: Oxford University Press.

Rees, G. (1993) 'Industrial change, labour relations and family structures: South Wales in the twentieth century', mimeo, Cardiff: School of Social and Administrative Studies, Cardiff University.

Rees, G. (1996) 'Making a learning society: education and work in industrial South Wales', Arthur Horner Memorial Lecture, Llafur: The Society for Welsh Labour History.

Rees, G., Fevre, R., Furlong, J. and Gorard S. (1997) 'History, place and the learning society: towards a sociology of lifetime learning', *Journal of Education Policy*, vol 12, no 6, pp 485-97.

Roose Williams, J. (c1945) *Young Wales and the future*, Welsh Committee of the Communist Party.

Welsh Office (1998) *Learning is for everyone*, London: The Stationery Office.

The necessity of informal learning

Edited by Frank Coffield

First published in Great Britain in 2000 by

The Policy Press
University of Bristol
34 Tyndall's Park Road
BRISTOL BS8 1PY
UK

Tel   +44 (0)117 954 6800
Fax   +44 (0)117 973 7308
E-mail tpp@bristol.ac.uk
http://www.bristol.ac.uk/Publications/TPP/

© The Policy Press, 2000

In association with the ESRC *Learning Society Programme*

ISBN 1 86134 152 0

Frank Coffield is Professor of Education in the Department of Education at the University of Newcastle. He is also currently the Director of the ESRC's programme *The Learning Society* (1994-2000).

Cover design by Qube Design Associates, Bristol.
Printed in Great Britain by Hobbs the Printers Ltd, Southampton.